# HIDDEN MOUNTAINS

## SURVIVAL AND RECKONING AFTER A CLIMB GONE WRONG

# MICHAEL WEJCHERT

**ecco**

*An Imprint of HarperCollinsPublishers*

HarperCollins books may be purchased for educational, business, or sales
promotional use. For information, please email the Special Markets Department at SPsales@harpercollins.com.

Ecco® and HarperCollins® are trademarks of HarperCollins Publishers.

Maps generated from CalTopo.com, reproduced with permission. Additional
copyright © www.thunderforest.com, © www.osm.org/copyright, © www
.norgeskart.no, and based on data from the National Land Survey of Iceland.

FIRST EDITION

*Designed by Angie Boutin*
*Image on page vii by John Gassel*
*Part openers © Design Pics Inc/Alamy Stock Photo*

Library of Congress Cataloging-in-Publication Data has been applied for.

ISBN 978-0-06-308552-7

22 23 24 25 26  LBC  5 4 3 2 1

*In memory of David Roberts*

DROP OFF

Denali
Hidden Mountains ○  ● Anchorage

BASE CAMP ●
MOUNT SAURON ●

PRETTY PEAK ●

ONE MILE

⬡ CALTOPO

a: John and Alissa's Position
b: Emmett's Fall
c: Lauren's Belay
d: Start of the Gully

DURING THE INTERVIEWS I CONDUCTED FOR THIS BOOK, I SOMETIMES encountered discrepancies in subjects' recollection of events. This is natural: Our minds and memories often betray us in stressful situations. I feel I have presented as accurate an account as possible, though I must also acknowledge my own subjectivity. In this same vein, I claim responsibility for any mistakes, however slight.

I have either omitted or changed a few names in this book to protect some subjects, both for personal and professional reasons. Most notable among these is Lauren Weber. For the same reasons, no photographs of her appear in these pages.

# HIDDEN MOUNTAINS

# PROLOGUE

In the summer, the sun dances around the granite spires of Alaska, projecting shadows here, casting light there, though it never sets. On June 23, 2018, two days after the summer solstice, the sun came around a corner of ridgeline deep in the Hidden Mountains, a phalanx of peaks so remote they had no names or history. Tucked on the far western end of the Alaska Range, the Hidden Mountains were thin needles of rock capping a wild landscape. The mountains promised nothing apart from adventure in a world where adventure was becoming hard to find.

The rotting snow and dark rock of the peaks always seemed to have a gray shield of cloud hanging above them. On June 23rd, though, the cloud bank had wafted out to the ocean, the weather was clear and blue, and the wind was still. If you had been a raven or a bush pilot and had dipped your wings in order to level off and stare across at one of these unnamed spines of granite, you could have made out the unmistakable dots of four climbers—two teams of two—strung together by neon climbing rope, the bright colors of synthetic and nylon jackets and foam climbing helmets contrasting against the dark rock. Bits of humanity enveloped in wilderness and quiet.

All day long, Emmett Lyman and Lauren Weber had been climbing in the shade. Finally, at around seven o'clock in the evening, the couple was rewarded by the sunlight as it poked through the spires. On the opposite ridgeline, two other specks of color climbed upward. These were John Gassel and Alissa Doherty. Occasionally the two parties whooped and hollered to each other, though the complicated terrain meant one team could rarely glimpse the other. The four climbers were close friends; both teams were couples. John and Alissa had even introduced Emmett and Lauren on a sun-drenched weekend of rock climbing in New York State.

They ranged in age from Alissa, the youngest, who was twenty-nine, to Emmett, the oldest, who had just turned forty. Each had successful, ambitious careers back in Boston, but they climbed as often as they could. Together they had traveled all over the globe, climbing frozen waterfalls in Canada, overhanging rock caves in Thailand, the desert spires of the Southwest. This trip felt special, though, because this mountain had never been climbed. So far as they could tell, even the cirque they'd hiked into—a snowy basin ringed with similarly untouched peaks—had never seen a human footprint. Seven hundred feet below them, the climbers' tents dried out in the sun, dwarfed by mountains that rose from snowfields and glacial rivers and the thick alders they'd struggled up the week before.

Emmett, Lauren, John, and Alissa hadn't planned on heading up this valley, but their original objective, a mountain several miles to the west, had proven too difficult to get to. They had spent four days ferrying loads of gear and crossing rivers swollen with snowmelt only to realize they'd likely run out of time to pursue their planned objective. A bush pilot was slated to pick them up on a gravel bar thousands of feet below on June 27th. But to the east lay another cirque of intriguing mountains, smaller and easier-looking.

Why not notch a few quick first ascents instead of one? Climbing was always better than *not* climbing, especially when they'd invested so much effort getting here. Short on time, they headed east and trudged up two thousand feet to this current group of mountains instead.

The mountain they chose from this ring was unnamed, but Emmett started calling it Mount Sauron because the dark, twin-tipped summit spires reminded him of Sauron's foreboding tower in *Lord of the Rings*. Sauron's summit was only sixty-five hundred feet above sea level. From where the group had crouched in their cook tent, melting snow and boiling water, the peak rose fifteen hundred feet above the snowfield. Rocky ridgelines swept down from its twin summits. Between these, snowfields eased back down to the basin where they camped, like the indentations between knuckles on a hand.

On June 22nd, the day before their climb, it had rained—the only crummy day of the trip. The foul weather had confined the couples to their tents. The gullies came alive with small, wet-slide avalanches, less dramatic than huge storm slabs but capable of knocking climbers off their feet all the same. Small rocks and debris bounced down the gullies, punctuating the light drum of rain against the tents.

But the next day, the sun shone clear and the two teams packed up, throwing climbing shoes, harnesses, crampons, ice axes, rope, and equipment into their bags and starting off. A tension simmered between them, if only a playful one. After all, whichever party reached the top ahead of the other would enjoy the distinction of being the first people to climb the mountain. Alissa and John had left base camp slightly before Lauren and Emmett. Now they were tackling the left ridgeline while Lauren and Emmett turned their attention to the right one.

Climbers use the same basic subset of skills to move safely

upward on rock, ice, or snow. A leader goes first, placing gear or protection: spring-loaded devices, called cams, which slot and expand into cracks; nuts that wedge into constrictions in the rock; and little bladelike pitons that can be pounded into small fissures. Ice climbers rely on ice screws, tubular devices that bite into the ice like an outsized version of a regular hardware-store screw. It is the leader's job to engineer the way upward. Usually the amount of gear placed corresponds to safety—so the more gear placed the safer they are, as there's more to hold and catch them if they fall. Modern climbers can rely on stringent factory tests that certify the strength of ropes and slings and other hardware, but a piece of protection is only as good as the rock or ice or snow a climber places it in. Engineering a good piece is an art form that ensures safety. This all sounds daring and risky, but most of the time it isn't. On many routes a climber tends to fall more often than they succeed, and they learn over time how to place gear to protect against those falls. In addition, a climber's partner belays them while they climb, which means managing the rope to help catch and safeguard them during falls. The partner also efficiently removes anchors as they follow behind the lead climber. Routes are broken into pitches, so climbers often leapfrog each other from belay spot to belay spot as they progress, pitch by pitch, up the mountain.

But there are still realms of climbing where a no-fall dictum exists: where falling is likely to result in injury or death. Ice climbing is one such subset. Crampons (the sharp points strapped to an ice climber's feet) and ice axes make for poor airborne company. And alpine climbing is another. Mountain terrain is often blocky and less steep than rock climbs, so a leader tends to hit more on the way down. And of course, a free soloist—someone who is eschewing any type of equipment, including a rope—must never fall (the trade-off for this extreme risk is speed, the unbridled thrill of moving without impairment). For the most part, ice climbers, alpinists, and free soloists choose objectives well below their ability levels in order to mitigate these risks.

Falling on Sauron would be disastrous. Much of the rock was crumbling and rotten and reliable protection was hard to come by. The closest true civilization lay across the Cook Inlet, a good ninety miles of mountain, ocean, and tundra away. Lake Clark National Park and Preserve, home to the Hidden Mountains, is not accessible by road. But the peak looked moderate—well within each climber's ability level—and as the day wore on and Emmett made his way up the mountain, he felt like he was climbing better and better. Early on, during the second pitch, a rock had crumbled underneath his foot. His last piece of protection far below him, Emmett had chided himself. *Hey, dude, pay attention, make sure you get your gear, don't do anything stupid on this, you've got to be careful, you can't have any accidents today.* But for the most part, bounding up a new route was just *fun*.

Discussing logistics in their base camp, everyone had nodded in tacit agreement. *No falls.* They all promised to climb as carefully as they could.

By evening both couples were high up the mountain, though John and Alissa were climbing more quickly on their ridge, about three hundred feet higher than Emmett and Lauren. Their options for descending were narrowing, and this sharpened their minds into a state of razor-like awareness.

Chasing this uncertain, fleeting feeling compels alpinists. It is why climbers return to the mountains. These moments prove difficult to describe to romantic partners or close friends, but the four climbers in the Hidden Mountains wouldn't have to. They were all here together. If anything, this experience would galvanize them. If Emmett and Lauren married—and Emmett, at least, thought they would— tonight would punctuate the rest of their lives. Climbing Sauron together would be something they'd tell their kids about one day.

Emmett had been in the lead throughout the day.

"He was just cruising all day long. He was in the zone. He was probably having one of his best days ever on the rock," Lauren remembers. There seemed little doubt they'd reach the top soon. The climbing was easy, although they moved more slowly than normal in order to not dislodge anything. They posed for a selfie at the start of a new pitch before Lauren settled herself onto the belay ledge. It sloped downward uncomfortably, but she'd leave this perch soon and climb up after Emmett, who was currently rearranging his gear before casting off on lead.

At first, Lauren paid out slack in the rope by watching Emmett's movements. But as he crested the ridge and disappeared over the left-hand side, she could only hear the muted jangling of equipment. Then nothing. The angles of the mountain threw sound in unexpected directions, and it was easier to hear John and Alissa, even though they were hundreds of feet above her. Lauren kept paying out rope until he was halfway, then more than halfway. He'd have to build a belay soon and then she could follow him up. With Emmett out of sight around the corner, Lauren relaxed a little and looked at her surroundings. It was eight in the evening. The light was brilliant. Her stance allowed an unmitigated view of the neighboring peaks, of the tents far below.

Suddenly Lauren was snapped out of her reverie by a violent, wrenching sound. She felt the rope come tight and knew that on the other side Emmett was falling, though she couldn't see him. Rock and debris flushed down the snow gully to her left so forcefully that it caused a small avalanche. To Lauren, the snow just looked like water cascading down, some unreal force of nature that still didn't seem like it was happening. Dust clouded the air.

Somewhere in this "I heard a human sound," she recalled. "It wasn't words. It was just a sound of . . . maybe surprise and dismay." The whole episode could not have lasted more than a few seconds, but to Lauren, this roar of rock felt like it had happened in slow motion. Somehow, Emmett had fallen, taking hundreds of pounds of rock with him. Lauren's position on the ridge, far to the right of the fall line, had spared her any injury.

"The rope got tight and eventually the rock and snow and stuff stopped coming down," Lauren said. "And then it was just dead silent."

# PART I

# ONE

In 1990, thirteen-year-old Emmett Lyman tied into a rope for the first time in his home state of Connecticut. His Boy Scout troop leaders parked behind a Mobil station and marched through the humidity, slinging a few ropes on an inconsequential boulder secreted somewhere along Interstate 395. Emmett and his fellow scouts flailed against the reddish traprock, wearing harnesses made of seat-belt webbing and yellow construction hard hats. Emmett was lucky enough to snag his mom's old Vibram-soled climbing boots, but the rest of the troop made do with gym sneakers. Chances were, if you tried rock climbing for the first time in the early '90s, your experience would have been similar.

Emmett was so smitten by climbing that he begged his dad to build him a bouldering wall in the barn, and father and son bolted a few four-by-eight sheets of plywood and climbing holds to the rafters. When he tried to start a climbing team in his high school, a single person showed interest before the effort fizzled. Three decades ago, when climbing gyms still struggled for a footing in the United States, these attempts were better than nothing. Options were limited for American kids bitten by the climbing bug: Either they lived close enough to a real cliff or mountain town, or, like Emmett, they figured it out on their own, rabidly awaiting the next opportunity to tie in.

If you had told any young climber back then that a climbing movie would win an Oscar, that gyms would compete against rival gyms in nearly every city in the country, or that climbing would morph into a billion-dollar industry, they probably wouldn't have believed you. In Europe, climbing has been ingrained in popular culture for centuries. But here, the possibility that the sport might be a hobby for anyone with a free weekend and an adventurous spirit is just taking hold.

In part, that's because Americans mainly obsess over competitive sports. It's easy for us to understand athletes who push themselves to the brink in order to beat someone else. We have a harder time understanding why—without any promise of riches or trophies or awards—anyone would travel to a mountain or a hunk of rock to plumb the depths of their own limits, even if it might kill them.

A CENTURY AGO, IN THE WINTER OF 1923, THE MOUNTAIN CLIMBER George Mallory boarded the *Olympia*, the sister ship of the *Titanic*, which was bound from England for New York City. In England, climbing was popular among Edwardian intellectuals and aristocrats. Having established and repeated several difficult routes in Great Britain and Chamonix, France, the tall, erudite Mallory was something of a minor celebrity, regarded as one of England's best rock climbers. But it was not until reluctantly agreeing to join the British reconnaissance to Mount Everest in 1921 that Mallory's fame surged far beyond that of cliquish Alpine Club circles.

Two years and two Everest expeditions later, Mallory was girding himself for a third expedition to the mountain that had become his obsession. The year before, as he led upward on a saddle of mountain called the North Col, an avalanche had killed seven Sherpas. It had been Mallory's decision to push on that day. He had assumed the benign slope would not slide. He had been wrong. In the wake of the tragedy, the expedition packed up and returned home.

If, as he steamed toward New York a year later, the accident still raced through Mallory's thoughts, there is little evidence of it. If the Sherpas' deaths haunted him, Everest's unclimbed summit haunted him more. The aim of this transatlantic journey, organized by the British Mount Everest Committee, was simple. In a few months, he and his teammates would once again travel to Tibet in order to have a third crack at Everest. This American lecture tour would help foot the bill.

When taken as a whole, Mallory's attributes conspired to make a great all-around climber. He married an unrelenting stubbornness with an athleticism that his partners had marveled at. But more important than his sheer physical skill was Mallory's acute awareness of the dangers of high-altitude climbing—and the ability to process these dangers, shut them out of his mind, and continue uphill. None of this helped him onstage. If he had expected rapt audiences across the pond, he was in for a rude awakening. His celebrity hardly spanned the Atlantic. The American public, it turned out, couldn't care less about mountaineering, let alone understand why anyone would return to stand on a useless piece of earth that just so happened to be taller than all the others.

"Mallory is a fine fellow and gives a good lecture," his American agent Lee Keedick wrote. But, he added, "the American people don't seem to be interested in the subject." As his tour wound on, Mallory found himself spinning yarns to half-filled halls. Events lost more money than they made. Wade Davis, one of his many biographers, wrote that "a failed attempt to climb a mountain evidently could not capture an American imagination." If anything, Canada was worse: An event in Toronto was canceled outright.

When his tour concluded in March, the dejected explorer waited in New York City, eager to board the ship that would carry him to his wife, Ruth, and their young family. It was here, in Manhattan (elbowing past patrons in a bar, some biographers attest), that a *New York Times* reporter posed a simple question—one no European muckraker would have considered asking: "Why do you want to climb Mount Everest?"

"Because it's there," the exasperated Mallory snapped, annoyed at the pluck of this Yankee reporter, whose name has been lost to history. Mallory's response has gone on to become the most famous trio of words in exploration. And if Mallory's quip lends insight about his own personality, then the question itself tells us how we Americans view climbing.

In 1924, Mallory traveled to Everest for a third fateful attempt. His teammate Noel Odell watched from below as Mallory and his young partner, a recent Oxford graduate named Sandy Irvine, willed their bodies into the high, thin air. From his vantage point, Odell squinted in order to make sure the tiny dots he saw were indeed men moving upward. In another instant, a bank of clouds floated in, dissolving the two men out of Odell's line of sight and into history. Though Mallory's body was discovered in 1999, no one knows if he and Irvine ultimately stood on Everest's summit.

In May 1963, forty years after Mallory's lecture tour, five mountaineers from the United States—Jim Whittaker, Tom Hornbein, Willi Unsoeld, Lute Jerstad, and Barry Bishop—summited Everest, becoming the first Americans to do so. But by then, the nation was too busy following astronaut Gordon Cooper's record-breaking orbit, the exciting final act of the Mercury Project, to pay much attention. In 1963 Everest had been climbed by two previous expeditions, whereas space was a new frontier—and a red-blooded competition with Communist Russia besides.

Of these five Everest summiteers, two, Willi Unsoeld and Tom

Hornbein, had done something truly remarkable—climbing's own equivalent of a space shot. Unsatisfied with repeating the route Edmund Hillary and Tenzing Norgay had taken up the South Col in 1953, Unsoeld and Hornbein became transfixed by a feature called the West Ridge. At first, the route looked impossible from photographs, but a snow couloir slicing down from the summit appeared to offer a key to the upper mountain. If they could manage to climb this feature, they'd complete a new route on the world's tallest peak. But the way forward presented a trap of sorts. At some point, traveling light and fast, they'd be too committed to the route to retreat. Salvation, then, lay in climbing up and *over* the summit, where they could reconvene with other team members on Hillary and Norgay's more established South Col route.

"At first the notion seemed, well, suicidal," Hornbein wrote years later. "Although the odds of getting to the top seemed low, in due course the prospect of a big adventure had at least some of us hooked." In order to succeed, the two would have to climb with as little equipment as possible, trusting their intuition and climbing finesse above any piece of gear.

On May 21st, the eve of their attempt on the West Ridge, Hornbein wrote slyly in his journal, "Tomorrow shall spell the conclusion to our effort, one way or another."

The higher Unsoeld and Hornbein climbed into the couloir, the more committed they became. Despite the late hour of the day, they strained uphill, overcoming difficult moves on friable rock and loose snow. At 6:15 p.m., they stood on the summit. The shadows of the Himalayas grew longer. Night was not far behind.

Three hours earlier Lute Jerstad and Barry Bishop had crested the top from the South Col on a separate summit bid (Jim Whittaker and the Sherpa Nawang Gombu had summited on May 2nd, also via the South Col route). As darkness fell, the two teams ran into each other and sat down for an unplanned bivouac at 8,535 meters

(28,000 feet), the highest night out anyone had yet spent. The four men warmed their toes in the arctic temperature of a Himalayan night, unsure if they'd sit down for good or rise in the morning, escaping that permanence of bitter cold and high altitude. Descending the next morning, frostbitten and exhausted and alive, it dawned on them what they'd done. Unsoeld and Hornbein had completed the first traverse of Mount Everest, climbing a new route in the process. Still to this day, more people have stood on the moon than have climbed what's known as the Hornbein Couloir, despite the hundreds of climbers who straggle to the top of the mountain each year. The ascent stands among the finest feats ever achieved in the Himalayas by a team of Americans.

Like the Mercury astronauts, the 1963 Everest climbers received medals at the White House and a spread in the September issue of *Life*. But then they returned to the guiding shacks and low-paying professorships from whence they came, while climbing burrowed back into the counterculture, the wider public remaining none the wiser.

Climbers reveled in this rebellious mystique, especially in the United States, where their deeds went mostly unnoticed. "In a larger social sense," Michael Kennedy wrote for *The American Alpine Journal* in 1989, "Americans view climbers as people engaged in an interesting and somewhat off-the-wall diversion—not as role models for their children."

The main barrier to entry was the sport's inherent danger: anathema to Americans used to suing fast-food chains over the temperature of their coffee. As the 1960s and '70s progressed, a subculture arose around climbing, featuring devil-may-care athletes with little to lose. Even labeling climbing as a *sport* was liable to get you into trouble with hard-core practitioners, who insisted it was nothing short of a way of life. When asked "Why do you climb?" at the top of Yosemite's El Capitan by a news anchor, the same question posed to Mallory decades earlier, a climber named Warren Harding screamed, "Because we're insane!"

Climbers sewed their own clothing and made their equipment on blacksmithing anvils. News of ascents traveled by word of mouth or in the few climbing-related publications. In 1972, the gear company Chouinard Equipment (later split into two titans of the outdoor industry: Patagonia and Black Diamond) festooned its catalog with paeans to using as little gear and leaving as little trace of one's passage as possible. Quotes by the writer and pilot Antoine de Saint-Exupéry and the master cellist Pablo Casals competed for space with fervent essays on this new style of "clean" climbing.

Armed with the gear Chouinard and other manufacturers now sold by mail-order or in new stores like Eastern Mountain Sports—drop-picked ice axes for climbing vertical waterfalls, harnesses that wouldn't break your ribs during leader falls, lightweight and removable anchors such as nuts and hexes, and a modern wardrobe of fleece, synthetic, and nylon clothing—climbers moved faster, lighter, and more fluidly over ice, rock, and mountain terrain throughout the 1970s. Just a decade earlier, it had been standard practice to climb up a route by using nylon ladders clipped to a piece of gear instead of climbing on the actual rock—a laborious and mostly mechanical process. Now young, talented, fit climbers, Chouinard's rallying cry echoing in their ears, tried to "free" climb as much as possible, using the rope to catch them only in the event of a fall and relying on little more than the strength of their fingers and the sinewed coordination of their bodies on rock.

The more you ratcheted up simplicity and uncertainty, the purer an ascent was considered to be. "It's the ultimate to go and do something and not leave any trace and not write it up," Henry Barber, one of the era's boldest climbers, attests. In 1973, the twenty-year-old walked up to a route called the Steck-Salathe on Sentinel Rock, then one of the most difficult free climbs in Yosemite, and soloed it on first sight, never having touched the route before.

Climbers could now take less into the big mountains, too. Peaks in the Alps and Himalayas had previously taken weeks or even months to climb. By the 1970s, small teams achieved similar results in days. The Austrian ski guide Peter Habeler, one of the first Europeans to visit Yosemite, teamed up with a young Reinhold Messner—later to be the first person to summit each of the world's fourteen peaks above eight thousand meters (or twenty-six thousand feet)—to climb Gasherbrum I, the eleventh-highest mountain in the world, in alpine style. The two mountaineers carried everything they needed in their packs, climbing a new route up the mountain in three days without any support whatsoever. In order to save weight, they did not bring a rope, soloing together, trusting instead their considerable experience and their new, Scottish-made Terrordactyl ice axes, which thudded into the peak's firm, steep snow with ease. Gasherbrum's first ascent, by an American team in 1958, had required ten people and weeks of ferrying loads up and down the mountain.

Routes on the cutting edge tended to be quite dangerous. Ferreting these new climbs out was also becoming difficult. Disentangling risk from difficulty, a growing number of climbers argued, was the only way to raise the bar going forward. They began drilling bolts into the rock to develop sport climbs on steep, previously unprotectable cliffs, rehearsing difficult moves ad nauseam. The old guard was furious, and during the 1980s, an ethical battle ensued between these warring camps.

In 1990, wearing his mom's twenty-year-old boots and a yellow hard hat, Emmett neither knew nor cared about any of this. Instead, only the simple act of moving vertically thrilled him. "It was this tiny little boulder," he said of his first trip out with the Boy Scout troop. "But man, I loved it. I thought it was so cool."

# TWO

Though he'd been born into an outdoorsy family, Emmett didn't climb on real rock again until after college. His parents, Dora and Emmett III (Emmett is the fourth Emmett Lyman), bought their East Haddam home after both had graduated from the University of Connecticut. Emmett III had been the president of the university outing club and the couple had met on one of the club's weekend trips. They had joined the burgeoning ranks of outdoor enthusiasts in the late 1960s, camping, canoeing, hiking, and caving together nearly every weekend.

"It was more of a culture thing back then," Emmett's dad notes. Though they dabbled in climbing, neither was interested enough to keep at it, preferring caving or canoeing or hiking instead. Emmett's parents stumbled on East Haddam in a happy accident, when they were both grad students at Rensselaer Polytechnic Institute in Hartford. They'd gone shopping for a cutting board for their apartment and had fallen in love with East Haddam—population 4,500—instead. Its rural, small-town feel made it seem like the right place to raise children, especially to Dora, who had grown up in crowded New Haven: "I'd always wanted my kids to have the same house their whole lives." Two months after this visit, they bought an old farmhouse. When Dora's mother saw the run-down place for the first time, she sank to the floor and began to cry. But Emmett's dad set himself to fixing it up, bit by bit.

Emmett was born in 1977, and his younger sister, Jessi, came along two years later. Soon the adventures their parents had enjoyed as undergraduates became family affairs. Emmett hiked the highest point in Massachusetts, Mount Greylock, as a five-year-old. Both kids camped and fished. During summer vacation, the family would load up a Volkswagen camper van and tramp around the American West, hopping from national park to national park. "We'd just charge across the country without a second thought. It was great," Emmett's dad says.

It's not hard to imagine East Haddam parents telling their kids to be more like that Lyman boy. Emmett studied hard and this devotion left little time for much else. Jessi remembers her brother in high school as a nerdy Boy Scout type—the kind of kid you'd expect to try (and fail) to kick-start a climbing team. When Emmett drove his sister and her friends to school, he'd blast the progressive rock band Rush on the speakers in the family SUV. Jessi remains amazed that he had a girlfriend.

It wasn't until Emmett went to Cornell that he dropped his Boy Scout bearing and loosened up a little. He messed around on the outdoor bouldering wall (one of the first campus walls in the country). And though he later kicked himself for it, Emmett never joined Cornell's outing club, despite the fact that its strong climbing program took students to the nearby Shawangunks, one of the Northeast's best climbing spots, each weekend.

His only Cornell experience on a rope was with his new friend Pat McNally. He and Pat lowered themselves down to the quad outside their dorm, and soon they were teaching a gaggle of dormmates and their RA how to rappel, too—until campus security marched upstairs. Emmett, gregarious to a fault, made a show out of displaying their knots and anchor (once a Boy Scout, always a Boy Scout). One guard who had some knowledge of climbing told the boys they'd done a surprisingly good job, shook his head, and decided not to confiscate their gear.

Emmett graduated with a double major in government and economics and a large amount of student debt. "I went to a good college and I was trying to build a career and live a life and find a girlfriend. All the boxes people tell you you're supposed to check," he says. That year he moved to West Hartford, Connecticut, an affluent suburb of Hartford. Aside from hiking part of Vermont's Long Trail with his dad, he abandoned the outdoors.

"I didn't have friends that climbed, didn't have friends in the outdoors. I kind of fell out of the whole scene," Emmett says.

He did the stuff adrift twentysomethings do after graduating. He bought old vehicles and fixed them up: a Jeep, then a sports car. He worked for Pratt & Whitney, one of Connecticut's two major aircraft manufacturers (Sikorsky Aircraft is next door). He learned to play golf "because everybody in Connecticut plays golf. It felt like I was stomping through the years, and it didn't feel great."

At a loss for what to do next, Emmett enrolled in graduate school, attending the University of Virginia for general management. Higher education did little to pry him from this existential rut. In 2009, when he received his MBA, the US economy was reeling from the housing crisis, and he took on even more debt. The Boston consulting firm he'd been interning for made a job offer on the condition he not begin right away. Instead, they'd pay for an educational program, such as language immersion, plus a little bit of travel time, as a bid to retain new employees. In September, Emmett flew to Santiago, Chile, to study Spanish. When his course ended, he headed down Chile's long, pencil-thin coast alone.

At the southern tip of the Pampas, the near-endless plain of

Argentina and Chile, the mountains of Patagonia burst upward. A visitor—*any* visitor—cannot help but be awed by the sight. The serrated teeth of the Fitzroy skyline brims with peaks named for the French aviators who died flying the mail up and down South America. It is so iconic that the company Patagonia uses the image as its logo. The contrast of the Argentinean desert to granite spires is one of the most awesome sights on earth.

On the Argentine side of Patagonia, in El Chaltén, Emmett hiked past Laguna Torre valley to Niponino, the last spot a hiker can get to before the striking peaks of Patagonia rise out of the Pampas. A few real climbers rummaged around camp next to a raging river, sliding their way on a line strung across the water. High above, Cerro Torre, the mountain Reinhold Messner had dubbed "a shriek turned to stone," shot out of the landscape like something from another world.

A glimpse of this skyline is enough to turn any dreamer into an alpinist. It is impossible to not at least wonder what being on top of one of those granite spires must be like. The notion that people climbed these peaks suddenly vibrated through Emmett.

*Up there is where life happens*, he remembers thinking.

# THREE

In 1988, a climbing competition was held in Snowbird, Utah, and filmed for CBS Sports. Some of the brightest stars in the sport showed up: Lynn Hill, the American woman who would astound the world two years later by becoming the first person to free-climb El Capitan's famous Nose route, battled to no avail against her French rival, Catherine Destivelle. Patrick Edlinger, another French star, walloped several American competitors, including Scott Franklin, the first American to climb the grade of 5.14.

But the most unique aspect of the Snowbird competition was the venue itself: holds bolted onto a concrete wall. At the time, climbing gyms were a rarity and the idea of transporting an activity like climbing, with its unique exploratory history, onto an artificial arena was a big stretch from the clean-climbing revolution that had exploded in the 1970s.

In the grainy footage taken for the event that still hangs around on YouTube, a CBS commentator asks: "What happens when all the peaks are conquered? When all of the peaks have been climbed? Where is the next challenge?" By today's standards, the footage looks more like a blooper reel for the movie *Dodgeball* than a climbing competition. But hokey, brightly colored Lycra and high-top climbing shoes aside, the skill amassed at Snowbird was remarkable. In the audience, Yvon Chouinard and Henry Barber watched this next generation take the movements they'd perfected on real rock and perform them in front of a camera for a crowd of around a thousand spectators.

It was no accident that the winners—Edlinger and Destivelle—both hailed from France, then on the vanguard of a new kind of climbing. Years later, the Snowbird competitor and writer Alison Osius noted: "Comps arrived concurrent with a sea change, the advent of sport climbing . . . the old order flung to the wind." Sport climbing had emerged in Europe in the 1980s, when climbers began using bolts to equip steeply overhanging routes that would have been deadly and unprotectable without them. Bolting a hard sport route eliminated danger but ensured difficulty. Now, instead of staking your life or limb on every move, a climber could forget about the dizzying expanse beneath them and instead focus on the intricacies of deciphering each segment of rock.

In many ways, this clean, graceful movement was what previous generations had sought, and while many climbers embraced it, it also made purists furious. A rift grew; friends chopped their friends' bolts and threw punches at each other, and debates raged in the columns of the two major American climbing magazines: *Rock and Ice* and *Climbing*. Bumper stickers that read "Sport Climbing Is Neither" adorned beater pickup trucks at local climbing areas. The soul of climbing, it seemed, was at stake.

Snowbird, for the insular and guarded climbing world, presented a face-off between the old school and this new wave of climbers. Many top athletes declined their invitations to the event, fearing a televised competition would sterilize and bastardize the sport. But as Edlinger (himself a daring free soloist) lowered away from the wall, the only competitor to top out in the men's finals, he pointed at Barber in the audience, whose solos had inspired him as a kid.

"*Pour vous!*" he mouthed.

"It was absolutely thrilling," Barber recalls.

"No one is sure what effect climbing competitions will have," wrote Michael Kennedy, the editor of *Climbing* at the time. "Many feel that they will only encourage more greed, selfishness, and commercialism in climbing, destroying the sport as we know it today; others see it as a wave of the future, injecting new energy into a stagnant scene. But, if, like Patrick Edlinger in Snowbird, we can preserve a sense of our sport's history and continuity, I don't think we've got a lot to worry about."

Looking back, Kennedy's take seems the most prescient. Those fretting over climbing's soul had failed to realize that training on bolted routes and in gyms got results. Clipping bolts wasn't some bastardized version of climbing. Rather, these tools were the key to making it accessible for everyone. And training and climbing in a safe environment meant standards were rising fast. Subsequent Snowbird competitions felt like rock climbing's version of the NFL draft. The name Tommy Caldwell would be on everyone's lips in 2015, when he and Kevin Jorgeson completed the first free ascent of El Capitan's Dawn Wall. In 1996, when as a sixteen-year-old Caldwell had bested a field of professional climbers to win Snowbird, no one had ever heard of him.

In the early nineties, around the time Emmett and his fellow Boy Scouts clawed their way up the boulder in Connecticut, gym climbing was taking its first wobbling steps in the United States. Though the concrete wall at Snowbird had been one of the first artificial walls in the country, other gyms began sprouting up—available not just to elite performers but to anyone willing to shell out a monthly membership. These spaces offered a gateway into a once-cloistered world; the athletic movement of sport climbing could be found far from an actual cliff, or even the outdoors.

At the time, one of Connecticut's two gyms was a teeny space called the Stone Age Rock Gym. As a Connecticut suburban-ite, I first tried climbing at Stone Age. I'm told the place is nearly unchanged today: Archaic by modern gym standards, it's pretty much a time capsule from 1996, just before *Into Thin Air* hit the bookshelves and I tied into a rope for the first time, a doughy ten-year-old in sweatpants. My old-school father didn't have a harness for me and refused to rent one, instead wrapping thick seat-belt webbing around my waist in a knot called a "swami." It must have worked, despite the practice having been pooh-poohed by safety-conscious climbers since the 1970s; if employees raised any eye-brows, my young self didn't pick up on it. I wore my mom's old high-top rock-climbing shoes. Textured paint had been slapped onto three-quarter-inch plywood, and bad classic rock blared through bad speakers. Chalk dust oppressed an already-stifling space. The owner of the gym, a guy in camouflage fatigues who'd nicknamed himself Kaos, looked like Rambo working at the local laser-tag arena.

To a pudgy suburban kid bored to death of cello lessons and hooked on adventure books, the climbing gym was the coolest thing I'd ever seen. Driving back to our little suburban neighbor-hood, hands sore, forearms burning and coated in chalk, I salivated at the thought of becoming a climber. Now it feels odd that that spark of inspiration—my first participation in a sport that has taken me to multiple continents, devoured my savings account, and com-mandeered my life—was ignited in an old warehouse between a dog-grooming salon and a Penske truck rental drop-off center. But back then it didn't matter. I had tasted forbidden fruit.

Three decades later, films like *Meru* and *Free Solo* are turn-ing mainstream audiences on to climbing. Podcasts and online training plans and festivals are growing the climbing community at a rapid rate. It's difficult to imagine George Mallory getting crickets in Manhattan these days. By 2018, the year Emmett and his friends ventured into the Hidden Mountains, the number of artificial climbing gyms in the United States had grown to five hundred, and American climbers spent an estimated $12 billion on climbing equipment and travel. A whopping 7.7 million people in the United States have tried climbing or consider themselves climbers, according to a survey completed by the American Alpine Club. And it wouldn't be unheard of for teenagers at your local gym to casually warm up on 5.12, the grade of the original Snowbird route.

All this means that climbers no longer have to live in scruffy vans or dilapidated shacks in close proximity to actual cliffs in order to practice their craft on a weekly basis. Today's facilities offer instruction, coaching, and comprehensive after-school programs. Kids go to bouldering practice with dreams of competing in events like the Youth National Championships or, if they possess enough talent and a maniacal amount of focus and discipline, the World Championships—or now even the Olympics, as four Americans did in 2021 when the sport debuted in Tokyo. Chalk comes in colorful packages that sell for sixteen bucks a pop (a shopper might be forgiven for assuming they'd picked up a pound of single origin coffee instead). Apps and online training programs chart progress, nutritionists parse diets, climbers record scores and route names on websites that rank their performance against their peers. A trained climber headed to real rock is poised to perform at an athletic level hitherto unimagined.

Those bemoaning the bygone era of painter's pants, beer, and traditional climbing love to gripe about their sleek gym-rat counterparts. What was lost, the old schoolers argued, was the *adventure* of it all: Hornbein and Unsoeld casting off into the unknown.

Accurate weather forecasts and route descriptions and increased communication shave off a lot of uncertainty from a climb.

"You know, you're being taught to move from yellow tape to yellow tape. . . . It's contrived," Barber opines. "I thought it was ruined way before [Snowbird]. Around '79, '80, or '81, when sport climbing really took hold."

But climbers like Alex Honnold, who grew up training in gyms before he free soloed El Capitan, or the late Austrian climber David Lama, who as a gym kid endured the derision of alpine purists before becoming one of the best mountaineers of his generation, offer pointed examples of climbers who have added vision, skill, and calm in the face of deadly consequences to the exceptional strength they'd garnered indoors. The future of climbing had arrived.

# FOUR

Arriving back in Boston in early 2010, Emmett washed his dirty backpacking clothes and buzz-cut his long, tangled hair. Instead of gazing at the skyline of the Torres he stared at a glowing computer screen for hours.

*Okay*, he told himself. *I'm me again. The old Emmett.*

He hated consulting, "other than the cachet of being the smartest guy in the room." Nearly every Friday night, Emmett would drive three hours to the White Mountains, home of the small, knobby Presidential Range, to hike and backpack, getting as far into the woods as he could before driving back home, arriving exhausted just in time for work on Monday morning. Each outing like this made the chasm between the outdoor world and the reality of his job grow deeper.

One weekend Emmett's buddy Pat McNally called, the one who had rappelled out the dorm-room window with him. Pat had just moved to Boston, and the Boston chapter of the Appalachian Mountain Club was hosting an introductory climbing course for members that would take place over the next several weekends. He asked if Emmett still had any interest in climbing, and together they enrolled in the course.

The AMC is well known for stocking and maintaining eight backcountry huts in the White Mountains, but it also offered climbing programs to members at a discount. That first weekend, Pat and Emmett tied in, learned to belay properly, and learned to set up top-rope anchors. Unlike Emmett's first foray into the sport, which had been a singular experience, the AMC classes offered a portal into a rich climbing community that had existed in New England all along.

"This is what it's about," Emmett thought during the first day. "We took the class, which was five weeks long, and at the end of it, we went to the Gunks. I saw the Gunks and I thought: Oh my God. This is where I want to live. This is what I want to do with my life. And we just started climbing all the time."

Quincy Quarries, the graffiti-strewn pile of rock Emmett soon frequented, certainly wasn't Cerro Torre, but learning to climb with the AMC was nonetheless a bridge between the corporate and the climbing world. Emmett and Pat quickly got memberships at the local gym as well.

AMC courses constituted a loose social hierarchy—there were a few "leaders" in the program, but the sessions often involved simply roping up with other course members and climbing. At crowded crags and climbing gyms, Emmett would run into the same people again and again. He loved this social aspect of it, of seeing familiar faces at busy cliffs, of going to slideshows or cliff cleanups, meeting people at the end of a workday. With each progression or skill learned, he crept closer to the proficiency he'd need in bigger mountains, but each step was also a world of its own to get lost in. The East Coast's tallest climbs are barely a thousand feet, but the terrain is so vast and varied, the weather so foul, that if a climber can keep their cool in nasty weather in New England, they can keep their cool on most mountains in the world.

By the winter of 2012, Emmett and Pat were hooked, and they

enrolled in an ice-climbing course with the AMC. The course fit Emmett like a glove. The AMC hosted one of its annual weekend getaways at Harvard Cabin, a dingy hut halfway up Mount Washington. Built in the 1950s, the crowded space had changed little in the intervening years. Staffed by a caretaker during the winter months, sixteen sweaty adults can sleep shoulder-to-shoulder in the bunkhouse loft and jockey for counter space in the kitchen below. Staying at Harvard Cabin has been a rite of passage for New England climbers for generations, for it allows easy access to Huntington Ravine, the small cirque and training ground where alpine gullies, mixed climbs, and ski runs snake down Mount Washington, the tallest peak in the Northeast. Huntington's gullies were some of the first winter climbs in the country, ascended in the 1920s by an eclectic mix of brash teenagers and old veterans like the British geologist Noel Odell, who took a tenured position at Harvard after participating in the ill-fated 1924 Everest expedition (it had been Odell who last glimpsed George Mallory and Sandy Irvine alive).

That President's Day weekend in Harvard Cabin, Emmett met another young climber enrolled in the program. The two hit it off immediately. Three years younger than Emmett, John Gassel hadn't grown up in an outdoor family. He was from Detroit. His dad had worked for the Ford Motor Company for thirty years and GM before that, and his mom archived medical records for the local hospital. John was an only child. He ran track and played baseball. He dreamed of owning a Corvette. He attended Michigan State and wanted to get a job in computer engineering, but in the end switched his major to electrical engineering instead.

If you'd met John on the street in 2009, the first year he showed up on the East Coast, you wouldn't have seen a climber. He worked as a bouncer in Quincy, Massachusetts; he had indeed bought the Corvette (figuring he'd rather have the thing when he was twenty-five than forty-five); and he weighed nearly two hundred pounds, the result of feverish weight lifting. But before moving to Boston, John had backpacked with an old college roommate around Glacier National Park. Halfway through a proposed twenty-one-mile loop, the pair was caught by darkness without camping gear. They hunkered down, freezing, before continuing on the next morning. Though they had exhausted their scant backcountry knowledge, they loved every second of it. John especially enjoyed the application of physical fitness in such a wild setting. He loved feeling out there and committed. He wanted more.

"We were total newbies." John laughs. "But it was life-changing." When he headed east, he tried indoor climbing, but found he wasn't interested in chasing plastic holds.

"It didn't really stick. Not that it wasn't cool, but I didn't get the bug."

But in 2010, looking for something beyond simply hiking in the White Mountains, John decided to take a three-day guided ice-climbing program offered by the International Mountain Climbing School, in North Conway, New Hampshire. Ice climbing—a frigid marriage of gear-intensive problem-solving, athleticism, and a wild outdoor setting—suited his engineering mind. That weekend, he and a guide toured the classic New Hampshire ice climbs, including one with the uninspiring name of Standard Route, at a cliff called Frankenstein. Standard Route has a much more inspiring signature feature, however: a cave formed by wild drips of ice halfway up. By the time John wriggled his way through, he knew he'd found something he loved—even if he had dropped some of the guide's equipment along the way.

While gym climbing hadn't clicked right away for John, ice climbing certainly had, and soon he was enrolling in the AMC's ice programs, same as Emmett. When spring came, John started to go to Crow Hill in Massachusetts to teach himself how to rock climb. "I did my first rappel and didn't die," he says.

Emmett remembers him as an all-out star in the ice program. John began lead climbing—normally a process that takes years of training—his second weekend out. But it was more John's personality than his natural ability that made him and Emmett close friends from the get-go. John was sturdy, with a muscular build, scraggly facial hair, and straight, dirty brown hair. His build seemed to reflect his personality. "He's unbelievably reliable. He couldn't be unreliable if he wanted to be, couldn't flake out if he wanted to," Emmett says. "And what more could you ask for in a climbing partner?" John took his climbing seriously, and he could be shy and taciturn at first. But when he opened up—and this could take a while—he was fun and goofy. Emmett loved that.

Around the same time he met Emmett, John kept running into a woman named Alissa Doherty at AMC meetups. She was obsessed with climbing, having found it in an even more roundabout way than John. Alissa had grown up on Cape Cod. Her parents had been very young when they'd had her and her older brother, and the family struggled financially. Her mother was a waitress; her father had been a commercial fisherman until the cod industry collapsed in the mid-nineties. He'd attempted a career in nursing but ended up battling addiction instead. By the time she met John, her parents were separated, and she was the only one in her family who spoke to her father.

It was perhaps this upbringing that had instilled in Alissa an unflappable resilience and ability to read others better than most. "The one thing about Alissa is that she's tough," Emmett says. "Beyond tough. She's had health problems and challenges and she battles through everything and you wouldn't even know. She is absolutely tough as nails. She perseveres through anything."

When Alissa turned seventeen, her dad told her she had two options: become a nun or start a family. "Well, I wasn't drawn to kids," Alissa remembers. She'd done a lot of volunteering with her father with the Missionaries of Charity, the Catholic organization that Mother Teresa founded in 1950, and he sent her to their convent in the Bronx. There, she lived with the nuns for a few weeks, working in the shelter the sisters operated. She rose every morning at four to pray.

"It was the most miserable experience of my life. I didn't want to go into this life, to take a vow of poverty. . . . It was the most depressing prospect to me."

In the convent, Alissa had a copy of Jon Krakauer's *Into Thin Air*, and she read it whenever she had any spare time. "I just became obsessed. I think the juxtaposition of reading that and being in the convent, thinking that was my future—the same day in and day out—contrasted with the incredible freedom and excitement and adventure from the book. Obviously, I didn't want to go die on Everest. But for some reason it captured my imagination: more clearly than anything in my life." Her new conviction was so steady that she even wrote down the words: "I will be a mountaineer."

Alissa relayed all this to her dad when she abandoned the convent after a few weeks. Her pledge to be a mountaineer was a different vow than what her father'd had in mind. But to his credit, Alissa's dad went all in, deciding to help his daughter fulfill this new goal as best as he was able. "Neither of us had any money," Alissa explains. "But I scraped together equipment." Father and daughter began taking hiking trips in the Presidential Range, teaching themselves enough basic skills to survive the harsh wind and searing cold of the White Mountains in winter.

"And so it was just me and my dad for the first few years," Alissa recalls, "doing ridiculously unsafe things. I don't think it was until my early twenties that I figured out that there were normal people my age rock climbing."

One of these younger people was John. On their first date, in the spring of 2012, Alissa led a moderate climb, well below her ability level, placing gear and scampering to the top with ease. When John followed, he was horrified: By his reckoning, not a single piece of gear she'd placed to protect herself would have held a fall, and Alissa had charged up, blissfully unaware.

*Okay, we need to go on another date*, John remembers thinking to himself.

Soon John and Alissa were climbing together all the time. Each saw a kindred spirit in the other, and they enjoyed the luxury of exploring this new world with a partner. Though their abilities were similar, their approaches were different. "I was much less technically competent than John," Alissa says. "He has an engineer's brain and I don't." But both Alissa and John were fixated on getting good at climbing, and together, they progressed quickly.

Pat remembers that even in these early days, it was obvious the pair's obsession surpassed that of their friends. On trips home from New Hampshire, the couple would recount climbs move by move. "I could piece together some of that stuff," Pat says, "but they had a photographic memory of climbs."

Another couple in their friend orbit, Emily Matys and Tom Miller, also remember seeing this passion on display while driving back from a trip to the New River Gorge in West Virginia. Dozing off in the backseat, Tom and Emily overheard their friends cataloging their climbs, section by section, and analyzing what they'd done wrong.

In the winter of 2013, Alissa set her sights on Mount Rainier's Liberty Ridge, one of the more technical routes on the iconic Washington State peak. "Liberty Ridge has the reputation of being the hardest and most-dangerous regularly climbed route on Mount Rainier," the National Park Service dossier on the climb cautions in its first paragraph.

Partly because the route is immortalized in Steve Roper's *Fifty*

*Classic Climbs of North America*, Alissa decided to give it a shot, even though she'd only been ice climbing for one winter.

"She asked if I wanted to go on this trip," John says. Alarm bells started dinging in his head, but John kept his mouth shut and politely declined his girlfriend's offer. Instead, Alissa simply walked up to a stranger at Frankenstein Cliff and asked him to go. That spring a third partner was procured from the bowels of an Internet chat room, and that summer the ad hoc team headed west.

Alissa had spent a lot of time researching the route, but the trip reports she used as sources were decades old. Climate change has wreaked havoc on Rainier, and climbing Liberty Ridge in July— the month she and her two partners launched up the mountain—is a nightmare of soft snow, loose rock, and miserable wallowing. Nevertheless, she and her companions tiptoed up to the base of the route with food for three days. The climb soon devolved into a terrifying exercise in suffering. One of her partners had diabetes and would slump against the snow every once in a while. The easy snow slopes from the route descriptions were melted into loose, dangerous bands of volcanic rock.

Back east, John hemmed and hawed. After five days, he decided to call the National Park Service to request the rangers see what was going on. A park service helicopter whirred over Liberty Cap, the huge glacier leading to the summit of the peak, and noticed three figures slowly finishing Liberty Ridge. Alissa and her partners were out of food; she'd gotten a black eye from a falling stone; they were two days late. But they were alive. In a sport where experience was as vital as fitness, epics like that provided invaluable learning opportunities. So long as you survived, making those mistakes would teach you far more than any guide ever could.

John and Alissa's passion for climbing was met and matched by Emmett's during this period, and he accompanied the pair most weekends. "He was our third wheel. But there's never been a better third wheel than Emmett," Alissa says.

John and Alissa on the summit of the Grand Teton.
*(Credit: Alissa Doherty)*

For this cadre of close friends, the week truly began on Friday afternoon. It wasn't unheard of for them to drive ten hours to some climbing destination, arrive at a campsite at an ungodly time on a Saturday morning, wake up, climb all day, hang out all night, and then climb through Sunday. Even Sunday nights, when most weekend warriors began the dreaded drive back home, Emmett would stay and soak up the climbing scene as long as he could. On at least one occasion, Emmett left the Gunks at two on a Monday morning, driving back to work in time to slump down at his desk. Once, a cop pulled him over on Route 93 in New Hampshire. He was going a hundred—a good forty miles over the speed limit—to make it to Mount Washington to start a climb on time. Astronomical speeding ticket be damned, he showed up in the early morning and climbed the route anyway. The weeks repeated like that. Clock out of work, get in the car, climb until exhausted, head home.

While Alissa and John focused on climbing the most difficult routes they could, pushing their own limits, Emmett channeled his enthusiasm outward. This often meant helping friends on middling terrain. John and Alissa would grumble to each other about giving up their time helping beginners on AMC weekends, but Emmett didn't seem to care.

"We whined to each other about days spent climbing 5.6. . . . We were always just a little annoyed by the shenanigans, and tended to look for the more competent new climbers. Not Emmett. I think he sought out the difficult students. He once spent an entire day belaying a 5.2 top rope in the Gunks so his mentee could climb it over and over and over. And he was so cheerfully enthusiastic, his climber had no clue that this wasn't a completely enjoyable day for them both."

Emily, who wasn't as invested in climbing as the rest of the gang, remembers Emmett always taking the time to climb below his ability level or to encourage her on whatever climb she tried. "He's always willing to help—no matter what grade you're climbing, he's always really happy to be supportive and cheer you on," she says.

"We fell into climbing and freaking loved it," Emmett says. "And at the same time, I was doing this job that I hated, and so that couldn't last long. The two were just totally incompatible. I would love to say I quit, but the truth is they managed me out because I was worthless at it." More than anything, Emmett wanted to climb full-time or pursue a career in mountain guiding, but he was so deep in school debt that he needed to keep working. After his consulting job was terminated, toward the end of 2012, he got a job working for Samsung in Ridgefield Park, New Jersey, figuring the town was equidistant to the Gunks and to Seneca Rocks in West Virginia.

That same year, Emmett fell in love with a woman at a buddy's wedding. Her name was Beth. She'd just graduated from Columbia and had taken a job with a think tank in Washington, DC. Emmett was smitten. For six months, he split his time between Beth in DC, climbing with John and Alissa in the Gunks, and working for Samsung in New Jersey. Though Beth didn't climb, she was a skier and was outdoorsy, and she soon began top roping and hanging out with Emmett and his friends at crags. But climbing was Emmett's "thing," not hers, and she never took to it the same way he did. Beth tolerated rock climbing, but she despised ice climbing. She felt it was more dangerous, a "gateway" drug to the mountaineering that seemed to kill so many climbers.

In Emmett's mind, he wanted it all—a relationship, climbing, a successful career. In reality, balancing these proved impossible. But he *was* serious enough about Beth that he planned on proposing to her, and he had even concocted a plan to do so.

In 2013, Emmett had moved from New Jersey to DC in order to be closer to Beth. The next November, John sent out a mass e-mail about a trip to the Canadian Rockies, one of the premier climbing destinations in North America. During the winter, the limestone walls drip with frozen cascades, transforming the mountain range into some of the best ice climbing on the planet. When he got the e-mail, Emmett was out west, slogging through another business trip. Canada seemed perfect. He'd propose to Beth when he got back, they'd go skiing in British Columbia for a week or so, and then he'd rendezvous with John and Tom to ice climb. How great would that be? He hit Reply All enthusiastically. But when he got back to DC, Beth was furious.

"You're not thinking about me at all," Emmett remembered her saying. "All you want to do is ice climb." And like that, it was over. He woke up and kissed her like it was any other day. Then she got up and left, and they never saw each other again.

Emmett was devastated. The winter trip with John and Tom in Canada provided a salve to the wound. They tacked their way up some of the coolest ice climbs they'd ever done. But once back home, Emmett's mental state deteriorated when he was suddenly alone in a city he'd never wanted to move to in the first place.

Emmett ice climbing in the Catskills in 2014.
(Credit: Peter Hoang)

"I went through a really, really, really dark period," Emmett says. "A few friends helped me through it." John and Alissa made it a point to climb with Emmett as much as possible, trying to bolster his spirits. And though they were still in Boston, they remained on the lookout for a woman who might share Emmett's passion for climbing.

Alissa's birthday was in August, when the white cliffs of the Shawangunks were illuminated by bright sunshine, and she tried to make sure she was there every year for the occasion. In 2015, a friend of a friend had tagged along. Alissa wondered if she might be a good match for Emmett.

Lauren Weber was in training to become a clinical social worker. A natural athlete, she'd mushed dogs and had a past life as a competitive swimmer. She'd enjoyed hiking and camping and had first tried rock climbing at a gym in Watertown, Massachusetts. "I liked the physicality, movement, and mental focus involved. And the climbing community in Boston is very friendly and open, so I established a really special group of partners and friends right away."

Lauren was intelligent and shared her friends' goofy sense of humor, but she cloaked her emotional depth in a fierce privacy that was part personal, part professional. Extremely motivated, she rode her bike twenty miles to and from work most days, often stopping at the gym to climb along the way. Lauren, too, had been through a breakup. Her previous boyfriend had walked out of her life as cleanly and completely as Beth had Emmett's. It was natural that she and Emmett would find common ground. The weekend of Alissa's birthday, the spark between the two was immediate. Not long after they'd met, Emmett flew to Florida to meet Lauren's family.

Emmett finagled a job transfer back to Boston and the couple went in on an apartment together as soon as Lauren's lease was up. They seemed perfect for each other, even climbing at similar abilities. Unlike Beth, Lauren was as passionate about the sport as Emmett was. As with Alissa and John, they found their strengths and weaknesses meshed well. The couples lived near each other in Somerville and climbed as much as possible, and soon the four were cavorting around climbing destinations in their spare time—first on the East Coast, eking out weekend trips and gym excursions as much as their busy schedules would allow, and then all over the world. The years passed that way.

In late December 2016, the quartet headed to Frey, Argentina, a rock climber's paradise outside the ski town of Bariloche. Serrated towers of rock jut up from an alpine lake. The climbs are short, just a few pitches or so. The airy spires are still mountainous yet possess neither the fierce weather nor the formidable reputation of Patagonia in southern Argentina. Nestled in between the bare, reddish volcanic granite at the eastern end of the lake lies Refugio Frey, staffed with a few locals—mostly college-age kids on their long vacation from school, which occurs during the December and January summer months in the southern hemisphere. Though the Refugio offers lodging to traveling climbers, most opt to pitch tents on the granite surrounding the hut instead, entering the hut only during downpours or snow squalls or to crack a bottle of champagne during Christmas.

Wandering among Frey's labyrinthine towers is a magical feeling. It's not rare to glance down from a belay perch and see a condor sailing on a thermal of air below you. The trade-off to this climber's Shangri-la is the approach, which winds upward through a dusty set of switchbacks. The six-mile hike isn't bad—unless you're a climber with a rack of gear and a few weeks' worth of food with you.

John, Alissa, Emmett, and Lauren planned on climbing in Frey around the holidays. Lauren and Alissa, who didn't feel compelled to spend Christmas with family, arrived in Argentina first. John, an only child, and Emmett, who'd never forgive himself for missing a family obligation, decided they'd fly out of Boston on Christmas Eve after making their obligatory family rounds. After navigating the gear-related interrogations by airport security, they hopped planes from Buenos Aires to Bariloche, which has a heavy German influence. (One scurrilous South American author posited that Hitler had escaped and lived there after the fall of Berlin.) As luck would have it, John and Emmett celebrated their arrival by heading to a German restaurant. In the morning, they'd load their bags and hike up to meet their girlfriends. But that night, John doubled over with that classic curse of international travel: food poisoning. Emmett, somehow, was fine.

As they waited for the guys at the Refugio the next day, Lauren and Alissa began to worry. Sure, every once in a while John and Emmett would drink too much and need a ride home from some fundraiser, or burn their clothes jumping over a bonfire, but apart from these juvenile shenanigans, both were the epitome of reliability. The Refugio had no cell service so they couldn't check on them. On that first day, whatever was causing the delay didn't seem worth hiking out to investigate, so Lauren and Alissa logged a climbing day and tried to push the missed reunion out of their minds.

A second day passed before John felt well enough to attempt the approach to the Refugio. But he had brought along a massive haul bag of equipment, figuring one grueling hike trumped weeks without little luxury items, and there was no way he'd be able to pack it all uphill in his depleted state.

For whatever reason, maybe some leftover masochism from his Boy Scout days, Emmett had a rare, sadistic love of carrying tortuous loads uphill. Now, with his friend in need, he decided to fit as many of John's things as he could onto his back for the approach, leaving John with only a day pack of gear to schlepp up to the Refugio.

So, on what happened to be Emmett's birthday, this odd couple staggered up the trail in comic procession: Emmett burdened by his hundred-pound load, and John burdened by the ravages of food poisoning.

Meanwhile, Lauren and Alissa's worry had eclipsed their annoyance. They'd spent a sleepless night wondering what the hell had happened to their boyfriends. Kidnapping? Had they just decided not to come? A thousand thoughts ran through their heads, along with some anger. On the morning of the second day, they packed up and resolved to return to the valley to unearth the whereabouts of their missing partners.

As they prepared to leave camp, a silhouette lurched up a rise and into view. It was Emmett, bathed in sweat and hunched over from his perverse load. Breathless, he explained what had happened, and Alissa bounded down to rescue poor John, who remained far below. The next day, John felt well enough to climb, and the couples enjoyed their winter break, the incident forgotten.

A few days later, over New Year's, when a pair of friends from Toronto, Canada, made the same trek up from Bariloche after having woefully misjudged their food rations, Emmett divvied up his to share. Even as his own provisions dwindled and he went hungry, he never let on, cheerfully climbing on far too few calories instead.

That was climbing trips with Emmett. Not only would he shoulder more than his own load but he'd trick you into thinking he was enjoying it. "A lot of times when someone dies or has misfortune fall on them, we say, 'How did it happen to such a great guy?' That's hardly ever true in my experience. But Emmett is truly that guy. He is just so damn good and kind," Alissa muses.

For Emmett, the act of sharing—be it a packet of instant soup or an experience—constituted a vital part of climbing. It had taken him a while, but he'd found where he belonged.

# FIVE

In 2014, shortly before she'd begun dating Emmett, Lauren was climbing at her local Watertown gym when she noticed Sharon Roberts, who had been her professional mentor. Lauren hadn't known Sharon was a climber, and it was weird to see her tying in. At first, Lauren was afraid to break the wall between her professional and private life, but she eventually went over to say hi. Sharon introduced her to the man she was climbing with—her husband, a climber and writer named David Roberts. Now in his seventies, David had spent his early years chasing first ascents in Alaska.

In 1965, Roberts and three other Harvard students—Matt Hale, Ed Bernd, and Don Jensen—worked their way up a knife-edge ridge on Mount Huntington, a triangle of granite in the central Alaska Range. Though lacking the height of Denali, Huntington delivered difficulty in spades, and the four young climbers toiled on the jagged mountain for nearly a month before summiting. Jubilant, Roberts and Bernd descended first into the growing late-July twilight. Suddenly Roberts heard an inhuman noise and the grating of crampon against rock. Bernd had somehow clipped in to the rope incorrectly before leaning back. As Roberts watched,

Bernd fell two thousand feet to the glacier below. Shocked and terrified, Roberts descended alone, waiting two days until Hale and Jensen found him in his little expedition tent. Bernd's body was never found.

The experience turned into his first book, *The Mountain of My Fear*. Such a frank confrontation of grief and guilt was not something climbing writers took on in expedition accounts of the time.

Not long after David and Sharon had met Lauren at the gym, David was diagnosed with stage four throat cancer. David and Sharon had not had children, and in Lauren they found a young person who was intelligent and vibrant and fun. Over time, as she met them at the climbing gym or for dinner, Lauren became someone the two cared for deeply.

Lauren would eventually introduce the older couple to her new boyfriend, Emmett, who fell in with the Robertses immediately. Sharon and David provided conversation and company and surrounded themselves with a wide cast of climbing characters, so the age gap never seemed to matter all that much. The couples grew close, and as David's cancer treatments intensified, Lauren brought him to appointments when Sharon could not. She and Emmett spent time with him and tried to cheer him up or provide inspiration during his toughest moments. They were willing to drop everything when the Robertses needed help.

By 2017, a few years into their friendship, David was lamenting about not returning to Cedar Mesa, Utah, home to some of the least traveled Anasazi ruins in the country. He doubted he'd ever see the place again, one of many possibilities that evaporated the more cancer took hold of him.

"Why not?" Emmett prodded. "We'll all go together." Lauren joined in. And so that September, Emmett and Lauren, laden with a double load of backpacking gear, labored out to Cedar Mesa with their friends. True to form, in addition to his own massive cargo,

Emmett snuck eight gallons of water onto his pack, just in case the spring next to the ruin was too dry, teetering under a load that was more than a hundred pounds in the desert heat.

David barely made it through the hike, but he persevered. The mesa was just as he remembered it, untouched, mysterious. "I sat on the bedrock where I had laid out my sleeping bag on a solitary journey ten years before and wept," David later wrote. The trip forged an indissoluble bond between the couples.

After a while, Lauren and Emmett introduced John and Alissa to the Robertses, too. "They're shy at first!" Lauren had warned David and Sharon before bringing John and Alissa over to dinner.

"They hardly said a word," David recalled. "I had no appreciation for how extraordinary they were when I first met them." Over time, though, they became close, and John and Alissa impressed the older couple with how seriously they took climbing.

"It seemed like the perfect story: these two couples in love," David said.

Though Lauren, Emmett, Alissa, and John had all come to climbing from adventurous backgrounds, they still stuck to known routes and objectives well within their weight class. David, on the other hand, was a dinosaur roaring from the depths, an ethicist lamenting the lost days when mountaineering meant going without contact for months, where the slightest error spelled disaster. He reveled in this role of curmudgeon, igniting discussion after discussion of where the sport was heading, refilling many a glass of red wine, everyone debating about what was left to be done in climbing.

"Nearly all the hardest mountains in the world have been climbed," David wrote in a 2007 letter in *Alpinist* magazine. "Every ridge and face in the alps or the American Rockies has been knocked off. Choppers called in by sat phones routinely pluck hapless fuckups from bivouac ledges where they would have died a generation ago."

"Why don't you guys do first ascents?" he began asking the two couples. The days he missed most, he wistfully shared, were those crystalline moments, cold fingers touching Alaskan rock no hands had felt before. Despite the great risk, that type of climbing had felt the most like adventure.

"In my day," he told his young friends, "climbing was about exploration!"

By now, John, Alissa, Emmett, and Lauren had climbed all over the world—they surely had the technical chops to pull something off. Why not seek out new routes in untrammeled ranges? Why let their skills languish at a crowded crag when they could be chasing glory on some wild adventure?

One night, when Emmett and Lauren were visiting, David pulled out a coffee-table book called *Alaska Range*, featuring a series of beautiful photographs and essays about Alaska's mountains: some climbed, most unclimbed. He opened the book to a double-page spread depicting a range of peaks called the Hidden Mountains. Serrated teeth of granite, backlit blue by the Alaskan twilight, expanded for what seemed like infinity. The caption betrayed little: "Sandwiched between the Revelation and Tordrillo mountains is a sea of nameless, unclimbed peaks known as the Hidden Mountains." An alpinist's Valhalla.

"Those have never been climbed." He paused for dramatic effect. "You should go climb them." Emmett and Lauren just laughed.

"I thought, that's not for me," Lauren says. "I like having a guidebook. And I like having a clear approach trail and a map."

Initially Emmett shrugged it off, too. The Hidden Mountains were too remote. With such busy work schedules, it wouldn't make sense to go on a trip where they could get skunked by weather or other conditions. Sure, the glory of a new route was great, but it would mean accepting the probable outcome of failure and a lot of elbow grease either way. But David aimed the same unrelenting drive that'd gotten him up his own first ascents into encouraging his young friends.

As a young climber in New England, I'd benefited from this guidance myself. David had climbed with my father years ago, and when he found out I'd grown obsessed with alpinism, photos of unclimbed Alaskan faces and old *American Alpine Journal* reports started pinging into my in-box. If David couldn't do it anymore, he wanted someone else to. During his illness, the thought of friends experiencing the peaks he'd loved took on even greater import.

"I certainly teased them about it," David says. "I still wonder whether I should have backed off at some point, said, 'You know what I think, it's up to you,' instead of exhorting them left and right."

David tried again one night when John and Alissa were over for dinner. Same book, same dramatic reveal of the Hidden Mountains. Except this time, the reaction was different. John and Alissa didn't hesitate: They were all in. The picture was a hard one to shake—that untouched mountains still existed, miles from anywhere. This simple fact felt like fiction.

"He literally pitched us on the expedition," John says. At first, in Alissa's recollection, Lauren was pleased John and Alissa had become the target of the Robertses' focus; maybe she'd be off the hook. But with John and Alissa on board, Emmett came around quickly. How could they not all go together? Lauren was hesitant but ultimately agreed. She didn't want to be the only one not going. "It wasn't what Lauren wanted," Alissa speculates, "but suddenly she saw that Emmett really wanted to go."

Emmett remembers thinking the trip would be everything he ever wanted out of climbing. At forty, he knew he'd taken too long to ease into the sport to become a professional, and he was too tied down with student loans and his career. But he felt as if this trip would be the culmination of the learning curve he'd embarked on when he took up climbing again. Besides, he'd get to go with Lauren and Alissa and John, and they could all experience the Alaskan mountains together.

"We all got kind of excited about this vision of exploration that none of us had ever experienced. Climbing had long since moved past the exploratory nature, toward crags and gym climbing," Emmett explains. "And it seemed like such a cool idea."

Perhaps sometime soon, Emmett figured, he and Lauren would get married, and maybe even have kids. Though he can't remember them vocalizing it, he anticipated these milestones. "I viewed this as potentially the big trip of my life," he says. "It's possible it might have been a jump-start to doing this thing more often. But it was equally possible this would be the one pinnacle experience."

Jessi Lyman felt differently. Her brother had been going on adventurous trips for a while now, but something about this one felt off. When Jessi and her husband divorced, she'd moved across the street from her parents in East Haddam. Emmett had stepped into the role of father figure, becoming more than just an uncle to her three daughters. Emmett would drop everything to help his nieces with their math homework. He made certain he attended each birthday party or first day of school. So over the years, Jessi and her brother had grown closer than they had been as children, and they spoke often. One day, while visiting Emmett, she saw him poring over maps of the Hidden Mountains on his computer. A certain bad feeling grew in her that she couldn't shake.

"I don't know why I felt that way," she reflects. "I didn't want him to go on this trip. And I said that to him repeatedly. I said that to him, even before he left. . . . I just kept telling him: Make sure you come back alive. I *never* would have said stuff like that to him. There was just something—I didn't feel good about it. And he kept telling me it was a trip of a lifetime."

# SIX

Few places in the world boast as many unclimbed, untouched peaks as Alaska. Many of Pakistan's six-thousand-meter giants remain shrouded in mystery, and countless new routes remain to be done on peaks that are off-limits to climbers in what was once Tibet. But Alaska is a cheap date for American climbers, absent of liaison officers or permits or even passports. Nowhere else is the inaccessible so accessible.

Climbing in Alaska poses unique challenges, however: bitter cold, remoteness, a seemingly infinite supply of mosquitoes. Those familiar with the area joke that it's "blue-collar alpinism." On some trips, shovels are used as much as ice axes and crampons—both to clear horrifying snow features on a route and to dig out base camps during the storms that blow in from the north every ten days or so. With no abundant water in liquid form, melting snow takes hours. The sound of a liquid-fuel stove hissing away is as synonymous with Alaskan alpinism as the climbing itself.

The central Alaska Range, where Denali lumbers above smaller, jagged peaks like Mounts Huntington and Hunter, is by far the most popular destination. Two key guidebooks serve as points of reference, describing scores of routes. Climbers from all over the world travel to the small town of Talkeetna, the jumping-off point for the Alaska Range. They wait out weather by getting drunk at the Fairview Inn, the town's most famous bar, along with surly locals and Iditarod prospects. Hanging above the bar next to the stuffed head of a musk ox is a sign that reads: "Talkeetna: A Drinking Town with a Climbing Problem." Even the most inebriated of tourists can stagger the expanse of the town in half an hour or so.

In the springtime, climbers rely on bush pilots to drop them off on glaciers swollen with a season's worth of snow. In the central Alaska Range, charter-flight services land climbers on flat, sweeping glaciers like the Kahiltna, below Denali, or the Ruth, below the hulking six-thousand-foot cliff face of Mount Dickey, the tallest granite rock climb in North America.

Landing a light aircraft on snow is an art. Modern glacier pilots still rely on rare, ancient planes like De Havilland Beavers and single-engine Otters. The antique aircraft are purchased from all corners of the world before being tinkered with and souped up like old cars. New engines are installed in order to generate enough lift to get climbers with mounds of gear out of the hills.

Flying onto a glacier is half *Right Stuff* and half *Beverly Hillbillies*. In order to take off on tarmac and land on snow, pilots have to deploy skis while in midair, often with a manual crank. Depth is impossible to gauge in flat light. Deep snow on a warm day can sink or flounder a plane. After snowstorms, pilots request that climbers stomp out a three-hundred-foot runway in the snow if they want to be picked up: ample toil for any stormy rest day.

Glacier camping may sound cold and miserable, but it's not if you're prepared. Veteran climbers jump out of charter flights laden with hundreds of pounds of equipment. To the uninitiated, glaciers are barren wastelands. To old hands, glaciers are refrigerators, freezers, and building foundations all rolled into one. Seasoned professionals hold the acute knowledge that no matter how hard the climb is, it's eclipsed by the crux of living on a sheet of ice. So they land with bacon, eggs, hamburgers, spare clothing, video-game consoles, booze, drugs, golf clubs, extra fuel, bottle rockets, lawn chairs. Nothing's too out of place, as long as it helps pass the time and make a climber comfortable. The mountains are cold, but the sun bouncing off the snow on spring days means a mountaineer is often sweating in a T-shirt in lower-elevation base camps.

Kahiltna International Airport, as Denali's base camp is jokingly dubbed, is the most crowded of these base camps, teeming with tents and a landing strip and toilets dug into the soft summer snow. On warm rest days, KIA feels more like a bar, bazaar, and airport than a desolate outpost. Recuperating there in 2014 after acclimatizing, a buddy and I watched one evening as a plane landed with a fresh batch of Denali suitors and their guide, whom they'd picked up, stone drunk, at the Fairview Inn. He was still wearing his flip-flops and a grimy pair of jeans, figuring he'd ask the pilots to fly his gear in when he was sober. My bemused friend and I watched as he stumbled from tent to tent, borrowing enough down products to swaddle himself against the cold while his inevitable hangover set in.

As glaciers have begun to recede, pilots have had a harder time getting climbers in and out of the mountains. According to some estimates, the climbing season has shortened by nearly a month. By the beginning of July, the stable snow covering big crevasses has melted and landing becomes nearly impossible; in a frustrating catch-22, this is when the temperatures are most ideal for rock climbing. Smaller, more remote cirques lack consistent flat glaciers on which to land a plane and thus climbers need to hoof it to reach those peaks—or shell out the extra thousand bucks for a helicopter.

Timing a trip is everything, but even taking the right few weeks off in peak season to climb in Alaska can't guarantee success. Outside of seasonal windows, there's also the daily weather to contend with, and few places boast such fickle climbing weather as Alaska. Sometimes the storms are slow-moving, spritzing snow at a gradual enough rate that it doesn't hinder progress too much. Sometimes, a ten-day storm wallops the range and even navigating from the cook tent to the latrine becomes a task of polar proportions. In hot weather, mountains tend to fall apart. Snow and ice careen down in massive chunks. The freeze-thaw cycles buckle loose rock, which reacts like a road peppered with frost heaves, sending rubble down gullies and off of faces. Sit on the Ruth Glacier on a warm spring day and watch the sun's rotation, and you'll hear a symphony of rockfall and avalanches ricochet off the walls. Depending on the snow year and temperature, climbers can encounter perfect névé—ancient, compact snow the consistency of Styrofoam, and a joy to swing an ice ax into—or sugar snow, unconsolidated flakes untouched by the sun, which coats ledges and makes for endless, horrifying uphill wallowing.

All of these problems aside, climbing in the central Alaska Range is pretty cushy nowadays: fly in, climb, fly out. With better, on-the-spot forecasting from websites like CalTopo.com and MountainWeather.com, a climbing team now knows exactly what's coming, for better or worse. Any layperson can click on a set of coordinates and get a forecast that's accurate within five degrees or so. Some deskbound climbers buy plane tickets at the last minute, flying in for just three or four days, nabbing a route before catching a red-eye back to the Lower 48 in time to punch in on Monday morning. If a classic climb, like the one David Roberts and his classmates established on Mount Huntington in 1965, is in good condition, it'll see several ascents in a season: a far cry from the monthslong isolation the first ascensionists endured. And a reliable scattering of new routes is forged every year by a selection of enterprising, bold climbers as well.

Plotting a new route isn't something many modern climbers take on, most choosing instead to follow a guidebook description, even in the remote mountains. Climbing has become so popular that setting out with detailed pitch-by-pitch descriptions isn't the exception but the norm. Repeating a route exponentially increases the chances of getting something done. The two Alaska guidebooks are now outdated compared to various online resources. For instance, the crux pitch on what is now known as the Harvard Route on Mount Huntington, which Hale, Roberts, Bernd, and Jensen had barely scratched their way up, now merits its own description on MountainProject.com, an online database detailing more than 200,000 climbs all over the world: "Vertical cracks lead up to a 30-foot section over overhanging green camalot sized crack, with smaller cracks on either side. Short pitch, 80 ft." Though weather and conditions still play a strong role in a climb's success, information helps to close the gap: previous trip reports, accurate topographical maps, and forums give a climber a near-perfect picture of what a route will entail. Gear left behind from previous attempts also makes descending easier.

Venture past the central Alaska Range and Denali National Park, however, and information becomes scarcer—and thus chances of success are whittled away. Many peaks don't have names, just an elevation marked on a map. Getting up in the air and looking out a plane window over the Hayes Range or Tordrillos or Revelations, it's impossible not to wonder which chimneys of ice or streaks of rock haven't been touched. But a new route requires time, planning, nailing the conditions, and luck. Heading to a mountain range that's never been explored is like a riskier version of trying to frame a house without a blueprint. You might be able to pull something off, but it isn't liable to be pretty.

BORDERED TO THE WEST BY THE NEACOLAS AND TO THE EAST BY the Tordrillos, the Hidden Mountains are tucked just beyond the eastern border of Lake Clark National Park. They're aptly named: unexplored and remote. Besides the physical distance from anywhere, the range is protected by natural barriers that make it a nightmare to get to, plane or no plane. Many of the small cirques are not large enough to land a climbing team on.

The Hidden Mountains were something unique in modern climbing, or even Alaskan climbing, a holdover from that era when alpinism shared more DNA with polar exploration than CrossFit gym culture. Instead of a well-documented mountain, here existed mile after mile of mountains that no one had stood on top of. Some of the valleys beneath the peaks hadn't even seen a hiker's boot print, let alone a climber's hands and feet.

"The rugged and remote nature of these peaks seems to repel any serious effort," writes Zach Clanton, one of just a few climbers to have explored the place. In 2015, when Clanton and his partners, James Gustafson and Tim Plotke, first committed to climbing in the Hidden Mountains, he spent hours in the air with Doug Brewer, the area's most active glacier pilot, just looking for a gravel bar big enough to land a plane on. The closest Brewer could find was twelve miles from the peak they hoped to climb, a trifling distance under normal circumstances, but worlds away in the remote, thick, dangerous terrain of Alaska. With heavy supplies for an extended expedition, the climbers spent five days laboring over those twelve miles. Bushwhacking here is a brutal art of its own. As Roman Dial, a legendary name in Alaskan wilderness travel who has perhaps covered more wild ground under his own power in Alaska than anyone else, reported after a pack-rafting and hiking trip in nearby Lake Clark National Park, "We had to wrestle and wriggle through brush at the pathetic rate of four hours to the mile."

In his reports for *The American Alpine Journal*, Clanton elaborated on the niche miseries of the place: "Incessant mosquitos and alders blocked our path and a machete was required to cut our way through the denser areas. Some days I would throw my pack down after an exhausting effort and see that we had gone as little as 1.8 miles. Some bears were indifferent to our passing, but others showed signs of curiosity and aggressiveness. On one occasion our only option was to spray buckshot from our 12-guage to deter them." When encountering such defenses was a prerequisite to even putting on a harness, it was no wonder most climbers headed for the central Alaska Range instead.

If reaching the peaks was difficult, climbing them proved even more so. While good granite swirled throughout the range, there was plenty of bad rock, too. Peaks as big as the ones in Alaska usually have their fair share of both: Bad rock often presents itself in stripes, a dangerous layer cake of solid and loose blended in a geological mixture across different elevations. Several pitches of fun, quality rock can be broken by rotten, crumbling granite with the consistency of gravel, as dangerous as it is absurd. Holds break; anchors are useless. One pitch you're climbing on the best granite of your life, another you're groveling up kitty litter.

On Clanton's 2015 trip, the trio made the first ascent of a peak they called Uyuraq, the native word for "brother," and launched an attempt on a peak they named Talliktok, which "ended in dangerously loose rock and very questionable belays," according to Clanton's report. The attempt on Talliktok yielded great alpine climbing up to 5.10 in difficulty, but the team was forced to bail after encountering a band of atrocious rock.

That year, the only mountain Clanton and his team managed to climb completely was Uyuraq, via a route the trio dubbed, appropriately, Silver Linings. The route was 5.7, an easy grade for the climbers but nonetheless an achievement considering the rock quality and the remote nature of the peak itself. Rock objectives in the Himalayas or Patagonia at least rose above hiking trails or glaciers, and climbers had porters or mules or horses to carry equipment. Here, there were no such options. It wasn't a stretch to call the Hidden Mountains one of the most difficult to get to ranges on the planet.

TO EMMETT, LAUREN, JOHN, AND ALISSA, THE THOUGHT OF GOING somewhere remote and unexplored was a breathtaking idea. Their previous trips to Canada or France or Argentina had always targeted known mountain ranges. This was different. All through the winter of 2017–2018, they divvied up the chores required to plan the trip into reality. At certain points, the whole thing felt more like a house of cards, less a tangible plan. Then, as they did more preparation, "It started to feel a little more serious," Lauren says. "It got more and more real."

John called charter-flight services, sleuthing out a few glacier pilots who flew into the area, and eventually he found a pilot who would take them. Unearthing climbing objectives without concrete information was difficult. No one wanted to fly all the way to the Hidden Mountains only to repeat one of Clanton's routes. Originally, they had considered chartering a helicopter, but those are not permitted to land inside Lake Clark National Park, apart from emergencies. So instead, they tried to divine the perfect mixture of accessibility, decent rock, and aesthetic beauty. Eventually, the team decided to explore a set of peaks to the north of the areas Clanton had visited on his trips.

Alissa set to work writing grant proposals, a job that dovetailed with her career in marketing. A few organizations, like the American Alpine Club, gave grants to interesting and creative climbing teams. In return the AAC asked for content such as photographs, video, and writing if the trip was a success. From a grant committee's perspective, two couples exploring an unknown mountain range was an enchanting hook, and Alissa received the AAC's Live Your Dream grant, given to climbing teams with regular jobs who needed a little extra cash to fulfill their mountaineering fantasies.

Alissa also applied for a grant from the climbing club Mazamas, a smaller organization based in Oregon. For this, she turned in a pdf portfolio outlining the trip—polished, neat, and brimming with photos of the four climbers hamming it up on previous adventures.

Lauren tasked herself with turning sunset coffee-table photographs into actual, tangible objectives. In his reports, Clanton hadn't posted much concrete information about where his peaks were. Yet through coordinates and clues left on the reports, Lauren figured out exactly where Clanton's peaks were located, toggling between CalTopo.com and Google Earth, virtually zooming around grainy images and double-checking longitude and latitude.

The climbers sent a flurry of excited e-mails to each other throughout the winter: "It's 8336 and looks nice and steep! That's 300' taller than Godzilla! Could that be the biggest in the range?"

Supportive, excited, and envious of his young friends, David

Roberts chimed in, procuring e-mails and phone numbers of local Alaskan climbers and photographers and sending encouraging proclamations: "Here, I think, is the last major frontier for great alpine climbs in unexplored cirques anywhere in Alaska."

Alissa and John weren't simply planning on leaving for an expedition; they were also planning on leaving Boston. Ever since their first date, the couple had dreamed of hitting the road and climbing full-time. "I'm probably the only person in the world who traded in a Corvette for a van," John says. All year, they'd worked on converting a Transit van into a mobile home, following in the footsteps of a new breed of young climbers who worked remotely from the road while traveling from one climbing destination to another. The Hidden Mountains trip was to be the launching point for this new adventure—an opening salvo with their close friends before striking out for more climbing objectives in Patagonia and the Southwest. The Hidden Mountains excited them, but the expedition also appeared as a singular blip on a long horizon of trips. And it felt bittersweet, a final hurrah before leaving Lauren and Emmett and striking out on their own.

Around the same time, Alissa got a phone call. Her father, who had been having breathing problems, had aspirated and died. He'd been living out of his van in the Boston area. Alissa was his next of kin. John was on a work trip in China the day she received the news.

Alissa was alone in the apartment when Emmett texted. Did she want company? No, she texted back. She was fine. Emmett and Lauren showed up anyway, and the next week, Emmett attended Alissa's father's funeral, along with Tom Miller and Emily Matys. "I had no idea any friends would come. Thinking about it in the years since, that gesture is the most deeply meaningful thing that a friend has ever done for me."

Alissa and John went through her father's possessions. They

rented a storage unit for a month and sifted through the man's life, piece by piece, keeping some things and selling what they could. They found a box with the hexentrics Alissa and her father had bought when they started to climb together, and they set these aside to bring to the Hidden Mountains. Alissa remembers the spring of 2018 as being the most stressful time of her life.

Lauren and Emmett planned on continuing their careers in Boston, so they'd spend two weeks in Alaska and then head back to their desks. It would be unrealistic to assume they weren't a *little* jealous of their friends who were striking off on a year of rock and ice climbing around the globe, while they slogged away at their jobs in Boston. In some ways, then, the trip would mean even more to them—and especially to Emmett. Buried with work, he wasn't as involved in the planning but felt he had the most riding on the adventure. He had turned forty that year, which he reminded his friends about constantly as they rolled their eyes half in jest. If he didn't do something like this now, he reasoned, he might never get the chance. He worried he was doomed to move from corporate gig to corporate gig without experiencing climbing in the truly wild places he'd been excited about in the first place.

But Emmett's calendar also posed the problem most likely to sink the team's efforts in Alaska. His aunt and uncle, who lived in Juneau, were hosting a huge Lyman family reunion that summer, and Emmett insisted he attend. Sandwiching the trip between work obligations and the reunion, the team would arrive in Alaska on June 15th and would have to be out of the mountains by June 30th. Two weeks left little time to account for the things that inevitably went wrong on expeditions—especially the notorious Alaskan weather. But everyone grudgingly agreed to this schedule, ceding to the powers of Emmett's boundless optimism that things would work out.

Each of them approached the trip—and their planning—

differently, and it caused minute stress fractures in their relationships. Emmett wanted to spend a weekend testing their new Hilleberg tents in the Adirondacks during a savage spring deluge, which was a chunk of time that John and Alissa—dealing with the loss of Alissa's dad and trip details and finishing up at their jobs—couldn't fathom taking off. Meanwhile, they had been sorting through numerous logistics for months while Emmett was too busy to help.

Of the four, Lauren seemed to be the most hesitant about the Hidden Mountains. "It was the biggest, most risky, most out-there thing I'd ever done," she explains. Technically better at climbing than Emmett, she was the least comfortable with the kind of alpine rock climbing they intended to pursue. Perhaps to compensate for this, she threw herself into preparing for the trip.

"It made me wonder if Lauren had her druthers, if she would ever have done that trip," Sharon Roberts says now. "I mean, she *did* do it because of her dear friends, and Emmett. But I have always wondered how much she really wanted to do it."

If there were warning signs about Lauren's hesitancy, Emmett doesn't remember them—or his own enthusiasm eclipsed her worry. "I think she was excited about the idea of introducing exploration into her climbing," he says. "She did the bulk of the research of finding this area of the Hidden Mountains and figuring out what it would look like, and she was super excited about actually doing the exploration."

"She had this training plan she was not straying from," Emily recalls. "I can't remember the logistics of it, but it was pretty crazy."

"She was being a little odd in the way she approached training and nutrition and planning," Alissa agrees. Alissa offered to go on runs with Lauren, who worried about her fitness. If Alissa slowed down, Lauren would be distraught; but if Alissa—who had done plenty of marathon-level trail runs in the White Mountains—sped up, Lauren would become distraught, too. "I didn't understand what she wanted me to do," Alissa says. On earlier trips, this tension had never existed. The two couples had launched out on their own objectives and each had been happy with what they were doing. But in Alaska, they'd be relying on one another in ways they might not have before.

In order to whittle down the unknowns of Alaska in her mind, Lauren created a detailed, ten-page contingency plan. If you could export safety to a pdf, this would be it. The document was stuffed with next-of-kin information, health insurance information, even medical allergies. Different colors differentiated responses to perceived dangers, which were itemized and listed according to day. June 17th to the 19th itemized hazards like river crossings or bear encounters. The 20th to the 27th listed avalanches on certain aspects or an accident on technical terrain as concerns. The number for the Alaska Rescue Coordination Center is included in the document. Everything the four climbers would carry was cataloged, down to the piece of gear or type of boots they'd be wearing.

When I tell Lauren that the pdf is something I would also put together before an expedition, she is visibly relieved. And it's true: I'm usually the one who prints out the maps and the phone numbers and lines up the grants. Climbers—or people in general—seem to fall into two categories: those self-confident enough to float through life with little exterior notion of a plan, and those who tend to lean more toward control as they make their decisions. Though partners of mine had always possessed a devil-may-care attitude, I'd always needed the assurance of as much preplanning as possible. It was rare to fly into a base camp without a three-ring binder stuffed with trip reports and other relevant information.

"I used to get almost embarrassed about being such a weenie

about these things," she tells me. The others internalized their concerns, if they had any. "If I hadn't done it, it was probably not going to get done," Lauren says of her safety plan.

Lauren made certain that each climber purchased insurance from the company Global Rescue, which partnered with the American Alpine Club, one of the sponsors of the trip. The company, based in Lebanon, New Hampshire, was a third-party insurance broker specializing in coordinating rescues between local search and rescue teams or other personnel and injured or stuck clients. They're used by everyone from expedition climbers to journalists needing a SEAL team to save them in Yemen. Membership with the American Alpine Club ensured some financial coverage in case of a rescue.

A key part of this safety plan was communication with the outside world. The quartet decided to carry two DeLorme inReaches, which are stripped-down devices that use satellite networks, allowing a climber to send a text anywhere in the world. Satellite communicators have quickly gained traction with adventurers looking for something lighter, simpler, and cheaper than a satellite phone. Compared to a VHF radio or satellite phone, an inReach is easy to toss in a pack. Now owned by the giant tech company Garmin, the latest inReach model, the mini, weighs three ounces—barely more than a Snickers bar. In addition to sending out a message and pairing with a smartphone via Bluetooth for easy texting, the inReach also has the capacity to send texts stamped with time and location—no cell service necessary. Family members may now view a climber's progress in real time.

Tom Miller and Emily Matys agreed to act as emergency contacts if anything went wrong. Soon the group was trying out the inReaches in their Somerville apartments: a challenge, since Boston has so few spots with a clear view of the sky. "Everybody humored me on that," Lauren says. "I had all those phone numbers, I had the

Rescue Coordination Center, I had the park service number, and preprogrammed all those into both inReaches."

Still, these devices were far from being a fail-safe.

In February 2014, a thirty-two-year-old financial analyst from New York City named Kate Matrosova became exhausted and hypothermic above the tree line in New Hampshire's northern Presidential Range. Rescuers dispatched to the GPS coordinates triggered by her personal locator beacon (a similar device to the inReach) wallowed through thick trees and deep snow in wind-chills that dipped to -100 degrees Fahrenheit. But the coordinates from the beacon had ricocheted off the complex topography of the mountains. These coordinates were relayed through the Air Force Rescue Coordination Center at Tyndall Air Force Base in Florida, but the device recorded multiple pings, which scattered efforts and sent rescuers a maddening triad of options. The morning after she triggered the device, a rescuer stumbled over her frozen body. With the windchill and fierce weather that day, it's doubtful a more ac-curate set of coordinates would have helped, but it was a reminder that, given the bad conditions often associated with rescues, even the slightest discrepancy could be costly.

Such inconsistencies in GPS coordinates aren't uncommon. Clouds and mountains obscure signals. The relaying of coordi-nates from local authorities to rescuers—a hasty, literal game of telephone—further muddies the waters. And the first-generation inReach (including the ones Lauren and John bought for their trip) had an even more insidious problem: The SOS button would some-times turn on without warning, even in a backpack. In 2017, two veteran explorers on a trek in Kamchatka, Russia, were surprised when their solitude was interrupted by the rotor wash from a Rus-sian rescue helicopter when their inReach had flipped a switch and triggered a rescue. Garmin, who had by then acquired the origi-nating company DeLorme, declined to pick up the $4,400 tab. So in an attempt to offset the chances of their inReaches accidentally toggling to the on position, Emmett cut a few pieces of plastic and duct-taped them over the buttons to create a homemade safety.

The inReaches allowed the climbers to text one another, their loved ones, and—most important—to call for a rescue. Simple communication such as this could have prevented the majority of the twentieth century's most harrowing survival stories: Aron Ralston pushing a button instead of hacking his own limb off; the Uruguayan rugby team sending a text instead of descending into desperate cannibalism. A few ounces of technology makes a big difference.

Climbers, for whom mounting a metaphorical high horse is nearly as intoxicating as summiting a peak, have had ethical concerns about communications in the past. Alpinism's self-reliance was a point of pride for its participants. Entering the vertical world meant assuming responsibility for the risk you were taking. You got yourself down or no one did. The famous Italian mountaineer Reinhold Messner chided his counterparts when they brought radios on Himalayan peaks. Being out there was thought to be part of the game.

Truth be told, the primary reason climbers didn't use communication past base camp often had more to do with practicality than anything else. VHF radios didn't work in the tight topography of many mountain ranges and most models weighed the same as a day or two of food and fuel. Besides, if you *did* manage to reach someone, the chances of being rescued were still slim. Satellite phones were also bulky, and most parties couldn't be bothered with the weight of one in their packs.

In 1989, Jim Sweeney and Dave Nyman, two highly experienced climbers from Anchorage, were attempting a peak called Mount Johnson, which rises five thousand feet from the Ruth Glacier in the central Alaska Range. They had flown in to the mountains without a radio. A pilot would pick them up in a week and a half and that was that. The arrangement was hardly unusual for the time period.

On April 19th, Sweeney and Nyman set their sights on the Elevator Shaft, a huge chimney feature on the northern aspect of the peak, a gash of snow and ice up an otherwise blank and impassible face. The route had been tried several times by a cadre of North America's hotshot alpinists and was regarded as one of the Ruth's best unpicked plums; so far, it had rebuffed all comers. The Elevator Shaft offered a natural line of weakness, but it also acted as a repository for debris—the obvious chute through which snow, rock, and ice tumbled down Mount Johnson's north face.

Sweeney led upward. At times the ice was good, but he also encountered unstable, vertical snow. On the fourth pitch, seven hundred feet up, Sweeney tried to navigate around a chockstone—a huge boulder wedged in the chimney. At first, he burrowed deeper into the chimney to avoid it. When this failed, he attempted to climb around the thing on the outside, but he couldn't find enough protection to manage it safely. For several minutes he hemmed and hawed, trying to decide whether to commit to the pitch. He decided to go for it and clawed his way upward, out and around the chockstone, getting farther and farther from his last piece of gear. Suddenly everything went black.

A huge shelf of unstable snow had given way, sending him into a horrible, ninety-foot fall. Sweeney came to a stop below Nyman, who rappelled down to grab him off the ledge he'd landed on. In the fall, Sweeney fractured his right hip and had suffered a blow to his head that broke his helmet and left him in and out of consciousness.

After rappelling with his injured partner, Nyman dragged Sweeney to the small, avalanche-prone basin between Mounts Johnson and Wake. Soon it began to storm. The narrow basin came alive with avalanches, transformed into a hellish trap. Nyman left Sweeney in his sleeping bag and skied twelve miles up the glacier alone to try and summon help. He stomped out a massive SOS in the snow. On April 22nd, a private Super Cub spotted the distress signal. The pilot decided to land to see what was going on, and—in a twist no Hollywood screenwriter would dare write down—crashed five miles away from Johnson, ensnaring the pilot, his pregnant wife, and another passenger in the unfolding drama. On April 23rd—four days after Sweeney fell—the Super Cub's occupants managed to alert the Alaska Rescue Coordination Center with the plane's radio, but bad weather precluded flying. Nyman, in an unprecedented act of heroism, had decided to try to save Sweeney by himself and skied *back* to the accident site. Reunited, the pair was battered by countless small avalanches. At one point they were washed into a massive crevasse. Nyman ultimately tugged the dying Sweeney toward the safety of the lower glacier.

Finally, on the morning of April 26th, Sweeney and Nyman saw a part in the clouds. "Just like in the movies," Sweeney later wrote, "Jim Okonek's red K2 plane flies up the middle of the Gorge followed by three military helicopters. Dave's crying. 'You're a hero,' I tell him. 'Get up and wave.'"

When the accident was summarized for the American Alpine Club's yearly report *Accidents in North American Mountaineering*, the pithy analysis was thus: "The decision not to carry a radio turned a potentially simple rescue into a major life-and-death ordeal for two very experienced climbers."

IN APRIL 2018, ON MY THIRD TRIP TO THE RUTH GORGE IN DENALI National Park, I carried an inReach past base camp for the first time. At one point, grappling with a dangerous, rotten ice pitch on a peak called the Eye Tooth, the thing started chirping from my pocket. Panting as I built a belay, I checked my messages: My fiancée, Alexa, wanted to know where I'd put the spare printer ink. The two realities—a technical route in the Alaska Range and printer problems in New Hampshire—seemed at perverse odds with each other. Such intrusions were new in exploratory climbing.

But to tell the truth, no ethical quagmire raced through my head, no thought of disappointing past generations. The satellite communicator didn't make the climbing any less dangerous. We still battled horrible sugar snow, we still triggered a slab avalanche or two. A fall still could have killed us. But it *did* make us feel like help was somewhat feasible, and to be honest, that felt great. That evening, crammed onto a teeny ledge with my two climbing partners thousands of feet above the glacier floor, I stared across at the finlike sliver of Mount Johnson, where Sweeney and Nyman's epic had taken place two decades earlier. *Those poor bastards*, I thought as I melted snow leaning out the tent door. *This stupid little device would have saved them a week's worth of harrowing survival.* Tucking back into our bivy tent, I wondered what we'd do if anything went wrong. One thing was clear: We weren't going to call for help unless we desperately needed it. Propped up on my elbow to keep our stove going, I texted Alexa to tell her I loved her. Then I turned off the inReach, tucked a Nalgene filled with boiling water close to my crotch to stay warm, sandwiched myself between my two companions, and drifted off into a cold, uneasy sleep.

WHEN ACCIDENTS AND DISASTERS HAPPEN, THE LOGICAL STEP IS to follow the trail of bread crumbs left in the wake to analyze what went wrong. At best, the process is a genuine step toward learning from someone's errors; at worst, a judgment call we make to convince ourselves we'd never be the ones to screw up. This is a handy rationale for participants in dangerous adventure sports. "Luck and skill: dear God, how the alpinist needs a boatload of both to get by," Barry Blanchard wrote in *Alpinist*. The margin between a glorious coup and a disaster is thinner than humans want to admit. And which side of the line we fall on is rarely in our control.

It's simple to criticize a team of climbers like the ones who headed to the Hidden Mountains. The easy conclusion is that the four—but Lauren and Emmett in particular—weren't ready to take on a trip of that magnitude, that they had little inkling of what was in store for them. The Hidden Mountains were a far cry from the civilized climbing of Frey or Chamonix or the Sierra Nevada.

Yet all four climbers were aware of their own shortcomings, not mired in hubris. "We're an unlikely bunch, we'll be the first to admit," Alissa wrote in the Mazamas grant. "We're city dwellers, weekend warriors, bound to our desk from 9–5, squeezing adventures into the paltry vacation time we're allowed."

When examined from another angle, Emmett, Alissa, John, and Lauren were well prepared. They'd done piles of research and covered many contingency plans. John had linked four loose committing lines on Cannon Cliff in New Hampshire in a day—a feat for any northeastern climber. Alissa had led plenty of poorly protected, heady 5.11 terrain. For their part, Emmett and Lauren, though less experienced, cut their teeth on terrain far harder than what they expected to climb in Alaska. The two had climbed less alpine terrain than John and Alissa, but they planned on ratcheting down the difficulty to counter this. "I mean, we weren't looking to do anything extreme," Emmett points out. "We were just looking to climb moderate ridgelines." Plus, having four climbers together offered a greater safety net for nearly all the objective hazards they were bound to face, from bear encounters to avalanches to enacting a potential rescue.

When I look back on my own first expeditions, long on psyche and short on real-world experience and knowledge, I cringe and breathe a sigh of relief; I'd scraped by. And perhaps the element we neglect to mention as often as we should, as if we do not want to admit it holds such sway over our own lives, is luck.

The cirque from the approach.
*(Credit: Alissa Doherty)*

# SEVEN

In the early hours of June 15, 2018, John, Alissa, Lauren, and Emmett landed at Ted Stevens Anchorage International Airport. The next day was a flurry of preparations: shopping for two weeks' worth of groceries, buying fuel for their stoves. That night, they celebrated at a local brewpub. On June 17th, they rose at five thirty and staggered to a Starbucks—the only place that was open—to wolf down breakfast and coffee before heading over to Regal Air for their charter flight. They spent the next half hour divvying food and cramming it into fifty-pound loads and tossing duffel bags into a De Havilland Beaver. At seven thirty, bleary-eyed, they climbed on board. The pilot took off and headed west.

Gray clouds hovered over strip malls that ended where the foothills of the Chugach Mountains arced upward. Some summits poked out behind a heavy cloud bank, though most were obscured. Of the four only Emmett had been to Alaska before, and the thrill of flying in a small plane above a landscape they'd long imagined cut through the haze of travel. The Cook Inlet shimmered to the southwest and soon mountains they'd stared at on Google Earth and CalTopo.com materialized underneath the low clouds. The peaks of Alaska shine with a reality that can catch you off guard, even from behind the Lexan of a plane window. Their pilot flew through Merrill Pass, one of the few places smaller aircraft can navigate to sneak through the western Alaska Range, and one of the more common sites for aviation disasters in the state. They glided past huge granite monoliths that rose from the spring snowpack.

The Beaver landed at Tired Pup Creek, a teeny airstrip to the northwest of the Hidden Mountains, unloaded, and left the group and all of their gear. A German ex-pat who staffed Tired Pup greeted them, as did his dog, who jumped up on the climbers while they waited for their next ride. A grizzly bear loped past on the far side of the runway.

From Tired Pup, another bush pilot would ferry the climbers and their equipment as close as he could get to the mountains in a Piper Super Cub—a smaller, nimbler plane than a Beaver—that had massive tires capable of landing on the loose, sandy gravel bars of the fast-moving glacial streams that flowed out from the range. The foursome couldn't all fit in the Cub with their gear, so it would take a few trips to land them closer to the Hidden Mountains.

At first, the pilot took John and Lauren up to scout out objectives. He kept his eye out for potential landing zones, while John and Lauren kept theirs on the mountains. But even from the air, the rock quality of the team's original objectives, on the northeast side of the little range, looked disappointing. There weren't any landing zones there, either. The pilot flew back to the west.

After landing back at Tired Pup, the pilot took Emmett and Alissa up next and circled around a set of mountains closer to where Clanton had explored on his second trip. To the south, an enticing peak rose up, buttressed by snowfields and topped by a striking, conical summit, an imposing citadel. There was even a gravel bar about ten miles away to land on. In midair, Emmett and Alissa made a decision and the pilot landed them on the gravel bar.

The mountains here were everything they'd hoped for—secret, untouched, unknown. A climber could show up every year for the rest of their lives and not even scratch the surface of potential for new routes. Emmett and Alissa must have pinched themselves. A year ago, these mountains had just been eye candy in a coffee-table book. Now they landed beneath them in real time, awed at the vastness of their surroundings.

When planning back in Boston, the four had hoped the pilot could drop half of their gear on the glacier so they'd avoid carrying it—a holdover from a different age, when bush pilots chucked packages of food out of the doors of moving planes to mitigate the loads climbers needed to carry on the hike in. Completing an airdrop was finicky: A pilot moving at speed could only drop off a bundle of food on a glacier with so much accuracy or miss so many crevasses.

Upon first meeting them in Tired Pup, the pilot, who had considerable experience in the range, told them that airdrops wouldn't work. With that, everyone's loads suddenly doubled: John, Lauren, Emmett, and Alissa would all have to walk in with twice as much weight as they'd planned. The nature of the trip changed in an instant. It stood to reason if the weight they all carried doubled, the time needed to carry it doubled too, and time was already constricted. Based on Clanton's travel time and the uncertainty of the weather in the range, the team probably now needed a month or so in the mountains to try to complete their original objective. But at this point, such a timeline was almost impossible. Emmett's deadline for his family reunion was already tight to the point of bordering on unrealistic. Still, if they had the weather on their side, they'd be able to pull *something* off.

After dropping Emmett and Alissa off, the pilot flew back to retrieve John, Lauren, and the rest of their equipment. The gravel bar he'd landed on was dotted with alders. Emmett filmed the pilot taking off, slaloming the plane through the thick bushes. In the footage, the gray aircraft wavers for an instant before weaving around its makeshift runway, its oversize tires rolling across smooth riverbank boulders. Suddenly the plane is airborne.

"Hell yeah!" Emmett shouted as the propeller echoed off of granite walls. The pilot soon returned with the other two and took off again, this time for good.

And like that, the four were faced with the mountains they'd salivated over for a year. In the ensuing silence, doubt likely seeped in alongside the excitement.

On the ground amid the team lay about five hundred pounds of equipment. Emmett eagerly shouldered a 120-pound load, swerving back and forth for fifty yards before crumpling in a comical heap. With much reservation, they decided the only way to effectively carry the weight was to divvy the loads up and double carry them all: going forward with one load before dumping it and returning for a next. Instead of hiking to the mountain, which Lauren had dubbed Pretty Peak, in one push, they'd have to carry loads as far as they could, double back for a second trip, and complete a second carry. This meant the hellish bushwhacking would need to be completed twice with heavy packs and once to go back in between. But with the hundreds of pounds of equipment, there was simply no other way. Even after splitting their loads in half, the packs were still heavy and the terrain was far from forgiving.

They devised a strategy in which one member would be left alone while the other three grunted through the alders, their packs bursting. Once the three could go no farther and shucked the crippling weight from their backs, one would remain in the vanguard while two returned for the one waiting behind them. In this way, they leapfrogged up the valley, hoping to find a spot where the river braided into a flow gentle enough to cross. Boulder fields and thick alders impeded their progress. The lack of movement was frustrating.

That night they fired up their Jetboil stoves and wolfed down penne pasta and hot dogs. Emmett managed to get most of it on his softshell pants, according to his journal.

After dinner, the team kept hiking their loads as far as possible in the eternal daylight, but ended up managing just 1.5 miles that day, about the rate of travel that Clanton had accomplished in adjacent valleys.

It had been a long day. That morning, they'd stood in line at a Starbucks on the strip in Anchorage. That night, they were deeper in the wilderness than any of them had ever been.

AT EIGHT THE NEXT MORNING, EVERYONE AWOKE. IT WAS AN-other good-weather day, though this hardly provided consolation against the mammoth, dreaded task of moving their loads closer to the mountains. The team faced two choices for paths forward. Alissa and Lauren decided they'd dive into the thick, impenetrable alders that make Alaskan bushwhacking so terrible ("Hell is an alder," Emmett noted in his journal), while John and Emmett launched up rocky drainages in order to escape them.

Above all, the group was terrified of bears. Before leaving, Emmett's dad and uncle—both gun enthusiasts—convinced the team to carry a shotgun in addition to the bear spray and air horns they'd already packed. But now the items felt like dead weight. There were plenty of bears around, but they took almost no interest in the climbers or were too far away to make any difference. On the second day, Emmett noted in his journal: "Lauren and John returned as we watched three bears amble past across the river. First a sow and cub—the sow was keenly interested in us, followed ten minutes later by a curious male that couldn't care less about our presence." The main danger came instead from crossing the river that thundered down the twin glacial cirques with the full force of spring runoff.

Rivers threading through the Alaskan mountains are swift and cold, fed by glaciers and snowfields melting in the summer sun. Sediment turns the waters brown, and branching streams braid and meander through alpine tundra or thick spruce forests. The rivers are best crossed early in the morning, before the sun has made its way around and melted the snow up high, but even then there's no guarantee of getting across.

On a trek out from Denali in 2014, my two companions—one a highly experienced Alaskan adventurer and the other a professional alpinist—and I struggled to find a spot to wade through the McKinley River. Out of food, fed up, and just an infuriating mile from the road after a month without showering, we paced back and forth along the bank in our thick mountaineering boots, prodding for a place shallow enough to cross. When we finally did, it was one of the most nerve-racking moments of the trip. Perhaps it was our exhaustion, but I hadn't realized how committing to the river crossing would feel until it was too late. Only once I felt the water carving into my waist did I realize we'd be unable to do anything if the strong current took us, except shuck our packs and swim as if our lives depended on it—which they did.

As they moved south down the valley toward Pretty Peak, John, Alissa, Lauren, and Emmett kept searching for a spot to cross. But every time they'd try, prodding their trekking poles in eddies, their legs began to freeze and then numb out entirely. They'd move on, hoping a spot would present itself as they neared the mountain.

On June 20th, their third full day in the mountains, John, Alissa, and Emmett hiked ahead with as much weight as they could carry while Lauren stayed behind with the rest of their equipment. In three agonizing days, they had thrashed a mere six miles from their landing site. Pretty Peak taunted them from across the stream, inaccessible. Each day that they struggled bushwhacking meant less of a chance of going climbing and a greater chance of "an expensive hiking trip," as Emmett joked.

But as they rounded a corner, they spied a snowbridge that had not yet melted. The river flowed out of that, so they could cross and get to the mountains from there with relative ease. Pretty Peak still seemed far away, but there was another ringed group of mountains to the east and these rose from a snowfield just a thousand feet above them. The snowfield would be a lot easier to ascend than the hellish alder hopping they'd just endured, and the peaks looked manageable, climbs they could complete in a day or so.

They were scheduled to be picked up by their bush pilot on June 27th. They'd been struggling toward the mountains for three full days. Like Clanton and his cronies, they'd been averaging just two miles a day—a disheartening feeling if ever there was one. And after climbing, they'd still have to struggle back, a process that would eat up an additional two or three days under ideal circumstances. This left a mere four days of climbing, assuming the weather would cooperate—not a given in Alaska. They needed every edge they could get. The mountains to the east were smaller than Pretty Peak and less striking, but there were several of them, and most important, they were closer. None looked like objectives that would make any heads spin back home, but at least scrambling up one or two of these would salvage the trip.

"What if we just went for those?" Emmett asked.

John and Alissa agreed: They should divert their attention to the mountains in front of them. It would increase their chances of getting something done. Besides, these little mountains still offered a crack at exploratory new routes in Alaska, which was what they'd come for.

They'd abandon Pretty Peak and focus their limited time on this new cirque instead. Once decided, John, Emmett, and Alissa hiked as far as they could up the snowfield before dumping their loads. Then they bounded back down the river to inform Lauren, who guarded the food.

Lauren had wrapped her head around the idea of climbing Pretty Peak. It was disappointing to not be heading for it now. What little they'd known about this mountain had been comforting. The new peaks were jarring, as close as you could get to an absolute unknown.

# EIGHT

That afternoon, the climbers left the nightmare alders behind and headed up the broad snowfield that ceded access to the small ring of peaks they'd seen. The mountains in this cirque were indeed smaller, with only fourteen hundred vertical feet of relief from the snowfield and just eight hundred feet or so of technical climbing. Much of the peaks looked like easy terrain—terraced, grassy ledges interspersed with alternating swaths of good granite and bad-looking rock—but if they stuck to the ridgelines there would be plenty to climb.

They picked a spot for base camp that was perched on a moraine fourteen hundred feet above the river, a small cropping of jumbled rock that poked out of the snowfield, like a jetty from a harbor, and overlooked the valley they'd landed in. As they began preparing their home for the next week, low clouds rolled in and it started pouring. Emmett and Lauren managed to set up their tent in time, but John and Alissa did not. Stuck out in the rain with the temperature around 40 degrees, the couple began to get hypothermic, unlike their friends who were dry and warm in their two-person down sleeping bag.

This annoyed John and Alissa. It wasn't like Emmett and Lauren to not help. It might have been a small thing, but the incident raised their ire enough that Emmett mentioned it in his journal: "They actually got pretty wet and cold. When the rain broke at around 10 p.m. we went out for water to make dinner and John came out for the same. He looked a little shaken, and we realized that they could have used a hand earlier."

The climbers had brought two Hilleberg tents for base camp: one for each couple. They had also brought a Megamid shelter, a pyramid-shaped tent that could be erected by lashing two ski poles together in the center and yanking the four corners taut against a snow anchor. The misunderstanding with the tents soon forgotten, John and Emmett set to digging out the snow underneath the Megamid, creating a trench and a platform on which to cook, a makeshift kitchen that would serve as a de facto common room for the duration of their short expedition. With their teeny avalanche shovels, it took a lot of work. "A lot of shoveling, but by midnight, we felt it was usable and made our dinners together. Around 1 a.m., we turned in, worked from a day of real exhaustion," Emmett recorded in his journal.

The morning of June 21st dawned blue and clear and everyone slept late, waiting for the sun to shine through the nylon fabric of the tents. Today would be a much-needed rest day. After the hellish approach, lounging in base camp felt nice.

John and Emmett trekked the fourteen hundred feet downhill to retrieve their climbing equipment, as they'd left the gear at the river crossing the day before. The nearly constant daylight meant that they had little inkling or worry about what time it could possibly be, and when they returned in the afternoon, John and Alissa napped while Emmett and Lauren read. For a few days, at least, they'd be able to enjoy the quiet of their base camp without worrying about much at all. If the weight of climbing new routes hung over their heads, it was countered by the immediacy of base-camp life, compartmentalized into a simple, pleasant routine. Their only concern was cooking their next meal or fetching water or sleeping. In the summer sun, camp was downright hot and everyone took their boots off, massaged swollen feet, and dried socks and long johns.

The position of the camp was wild, perched on a moraine perhaps no one had even stood on top of before. In all the climbing trips they'd taken, other climbers or hikers had hovered alongside them in the campsites or alpine meadows. No matter how remote they'd gotten, it hadn't come close to this kind of wilderness.

Later that afternoon, the weather closed in again and it began to rain. At around six, Lauren and Emmett donned their snowshoes and hiked up and down the cirque, staring at objectives. The cirque itself was just over half a mile long and the peaks that loomed were only a thousand feet or so. "Overall rock quality left a lot to be desired," Emmett wrote.

Up close, these little mountains weren't as striking as the ones they'd obsessed over on Google Earth. But still, *some* climbing was better than none. If even one of them got to the top of anything new, it would be an accomplishment. The hike in had been worse than any of them imagined, but they'd done it. Plenty of climbing expeditions had failed to even make it to the mountains, so thus far theirs felt like a success. Plenty of expeditions, too, had ended up following similar contingency plans instead of the original objective. And if nothing else, they had learned valuable lessons about the Hidden Mountains for a return trip, perhaps the following year.

Small wet slide avalanches sloughed down from the gullies above them. There was nothing huge coming down, but it unnerved them. In the winter, when the mountains receive less sun, snow accumulates in layers, like a cake, settling with wind and hanging on to the slopes. Avalanches most often occur on slopes of between thirty and forty-five degrees. Any steeper than that and new snow simply sloughs off before it accumulates; any lower than that and a slope isn't steep enough to slide.

In the summertime, slopes have "rounded," as avalanche forecasters say, meaning the different layers are hit by the sun, melt, and settle into one another, congealing into amorphous glop that's generally safe. But in spring and summer when mountains heat up too much—as the cirque was now doing during the longest day of the year—the mountains shed a layer of slush.

The warmth meant rockfall was a danger, too, as the sudden fluctuation in temperature heaved the peaks apart. By all scant accounts, the rock in the Hidden Mountains was not good. Bands of bad granite precluded Clanton from summiting any of his major objectives on his first trip; the cirque Emmett had picked likewise looked rotten. Each hold would have to be tested carefully; each movement and placement would need a cautious evaluation.

To alleviate these dangers, Lauren and Emmett planned on trying the southernmost peak in their little ring of mountains, a twin-tipped summit Emmett had dubbed Mount Sauron, because it looked just like the forked peak from *The Lord of the Rings*. The peak had two obvious ridges on the left and right side. Between these, a massive snow gully split the mountain in two. Wet slides came down this natural funnel every once in a while, but if Lauren and Emmett stayed on a ridge, they'd be safe enough.

For climbers, ridges offer natural aspects of safety and it is no accident that ridgelines are usually the first features climbed on a virgin peak. Snow, ice, and cornices tend to fall to one side or the other, down concave faces and into drainages. Though Sauron's left-hand ridgeline ended in a steep headwall, the right-hand ridge appeared to offer a jumbled, moderate line to the summit. If the rock was as bad as it looked, at least the ridge climbing would be low angle and easy enough to mitigate the risk.

To Lauren, the shift of objectives wasn't ideal. On the reconnaissance flight, Alissa and Emmett had gotten a good look at the granite on Pretty Peak. But the rock in this new cirque was questionable, a plan thrown suddenly off-kilter. "We didn't have any knowledge of this new one," Lauren remembers. "That was disconcerting, for sure."

Sauron was a contingency plan through and through: not quite so striking, not nearly as difficult as anyone had hoped. But someday they'd be back to these mountains, they reasoned, to try another objective.

On June 22nd, the weather remained unsettled and everyone stayed close to base camp. John sent a message to David and Sharon Roberts that night on their inReach: "Hello from base camp, friends! Forgive us this contact to the outside world but weather is looking magnificent tomorrow and we're excited for what lies ahead. . . . We have many stories to share when we reconvene ☺!"

John and Alissa, after also scouting up and down the cirque, had decided on attempting the left ridge of Sauron. This line looked more difficult, but it seemed to have some of the cleanest and best rock out of their options.

That evening in the cook tent, Emmett and Lauren announced they'd attempt the right-hand skyline, and John and Alissa voiced their desire to try the left-hand one. Climbing two routes on Sauron also made practical sense. If both teams were on the same mountain, they reasoned, they could pool their resources to get down—they'd have twice as many ropes and twice as much gear with which to enact a retreat. Besides, if anything went wrong, four people on a mountain meant far more security than just two.

Emmett proposed waiting until much later in the day to start up the mountain. With constant daylight, there was little sense in getting an alpine start. The mountain's northeast face only came into the sun at around five thirty in the evening. If they waited, they'd be able to climb in the sun instead of freezing in the morning shade. But in the end, everyone agreed on an earlier start, leaving camp around seven a.m. Everyone agreed, too, to turn back if things became too difficult. With the looseness of the terrain, they simply couldn't risk falls.

Later that night, back in their own tent, John and Alissa lay next to each other in their shared sleeping bag. Before the trip, they'd each read *The Tower*, Kelly Cordes's sweeping, passionate history of climbing on Cerro Torre in Patagonia. They dreamed of heading down to Patagonia themselves later that year and were rabidly devouring any information they could find on the place.

Toward the end of the book, Cordes recounts the death of the twenty-nine-year-old Canadian Carlyle Norman on another peak in the range, Aguja Saint-Exupéry. Norman's partner, a fellow Canadian named Cian Brinker, had accidentally pulled down a massive chunk of rock that had critically injured her.

Brinker "had three choices," Cordes wrote. "He could try to bring Norman down—a desperate proposition with an unresponsive and gravely injured person, especially given the broken terrain and loose blocks on the ledges. He could stay with her, but dying beside her would serve no purpose. Or, perhaps most excruciating, he could leave her and go for help."

He descended alone and hiked out to the town El Chaltén—a two-day odyssey—and alerted local entities. A small team of crack climbers assembled quickly (there is only a volunteer rescue team in the town, but there are always a handful of elite alpinists milling around El Chaltén) and a film crew loaned a helicopter to ferry rescuers to the base of Saint-Exupéry and determine Norman's position and condition, though it couldn't land and had no winch to lower a rescuer. The helicopter's footage showed that Norman, perhaps semiconscious, had tried to descend, getting herself to another ledge about forty feet down from the site of the accident, where she now lay crumpled and unresponsive. But as they scanned the footage, the helicopter crew thought they'd seen Norman's arm move.

Racing an incoming storm and darkness, four alpinists battled upward to try and reach Norman, climbing through sleet and snow, soon by the light of their headlamps. After a frigid bivy, and unsure if, in her vastly deteriorated state, Norman could have survived such a hellish night in the open, the rescuers retreated, hoping to return in better weather. The rescuers had accrued "more risk than any of them would assume in their own climbing," as Cordes puts it.

Five days after the accident, in better weather, the helicopter flew back over the ridge where Norman had last been seen. On board was one of the original rescuers, a bold American climber named Colin Haley, and the Canadian climber and filmmaker Josh Lavigne, who had dated Norman for years and had flown down from Canada to assist in any way he could.

Hovering overhead, they realized she was gone. She must have fallen or dragged herself over the ledge. Later, Lavigne hiked up to the glacier underneath Saint-Exupéry, retrieving what he could of her human remains and burying them under a cairn at the toe of the Rio Blanco glacier. As an orphan, Norman's worst fear had been abandonment.

On the night of June 22nd, before going to sleep, John and Alissa made a kind of pact. It probably seemed silly. But if something happened to any of them, the others would do their best to make sure they weren't alone.

# NINE

On the morning of June 23rd, the bad weather cleared. Apart from a few wisps of clouds that glided toward the coast, the mountains were still. Everyone had risen early, churning with a mixture of excitement and nerves. Mountaineers love mornings, once they get going. Rising into action in the stiff cold is better than waiting in the tent, sleepless and full of doubt. The anticipation cedes to movement and movement is simple.

The view expanded as the clouds lifted from their camp, and from this vantage point, on the precipice of moraine and snowfield, the climbers could again see the valley they'd trudged up. The terrain stretched north down the valley, toward the gray-green of the alders and spruce and the river rushing down, dark and strewn with silt.

It was cold for rock climbing, around 40 degrees Fahrenheit, and the sun wouldn't reach them for hours. They stumbled out of their tents with chilly hands and vapor on their breath. Soon, the routine of preparation interrupted the silence of the place. It was not spoken of in the moment, but there was a light competition to see who would leave camp first.

Emmett packing for the climb.
(Credit: Alissa Doherty)

Breakfast was wolfed down, bowels had to be emptied. Water was melted from snow and packs were readied. No matter how much packing a climber does the night before, there are always last-minute adjustments: lip balm or a tube of sunscreen tossed in a pocket, an extra carabiner for a jacket clipped onto a harness. A photograph of the route snapped on a phone, tent zippers opened and closed until it's past time to leave.

Because of preprogrammed updates on their inReaches, John, Alissa, Lauren, and Emmett knew the weather would be relatively stable all day—a ten percent chance of precipitation, partly sunny. A little raindrop icon on the device hovered over that night, but better weather followed. They planned on finishing by evening, anyway. Packing light, the two teams didn't carry any kind of bivouac gear such as a stove or a lightweight tarp to huddle under in the cold predawn hours if they became stranded up on the wall. Every extra ounce a climber carries adds unnecessary weight to a body straining to move upward. The climb would take a day, they reasoned. Maybe a long one. But a day.

Each party had a light rock rack: a full set of cams, nuts, and hexentrics. The hexes were Alissa's father's. They were practical items, but they also tied this trip to her dad and to how she'd learned to climb. Each team also brought a hammer for banging in pitons; David Roberts had loaned one to each couple before they left Boston. The hammers had driven home plenty of pins in Alaska. Apart from being another keepsake item, they were useful, too; the climbing company Black Diamond still sells its original hammer design from 1972 on its website.

Everyone hoped to climb in their mountaineering boots as much as possible. Boots were warm and comfortable and rock shoes were not. Each climber brought little backpacks for essential items—

water, some energy bars, a few warm layers—but they omitted a first aid kit to save weight.

John and Alissa left base camp first, hiking with their snow-shoes on. They plodded up the arcing snowfield, threading their way between the two cones of debris that had washed down the gullies during the rainy day before. The wet slides had deposited the snow in clumps along with rocks and moss and detritus from the mountain, staining the snow black and gray, the color of the rock buttresses from where they'd fallen. Below them, Lauren and Emmett followed around twenty minutes later, red and blue dots on the snowfield, tracing their friends' snowshoe tracks until they branched off to the right to the ridge they'd spied the previous day.

The rhythm of climbing—the cadence of movement, of upward momentum—is an elusive thing, and the slightest spasm in a mental muscle can throw it off. Above all else, climbers battle for control. This does not mean supremacy over the environment so much as the idea that choices exist, that a climber may keep making decisions to drive their movements in one way or another. In the early moments of a long climb, and especially a new climb, the day is shrouded by gnawing uncertainty. Experienced climbers learn to do a few things: recognize what are real concerns—avalanche hazards, bad rock, the time of day—and separate these real concerns from perceived fear, the mental tricks we all play when we begin doubting ourselves. When these fears are eclipsed, when they are replaced by those moments of control, and when that control turns into a kind of grace—this is what climbers savor and what they will remember long after a climb is finished.

The foursome had come in pursuit of this grace, this rhythm.

No matter what, though, it's hard to shake the cobwebs out, to transition from the uncertainty of lying in a sleeping bag, or staring up at a route, to the action of the thing. But then hands touch rock, boots kick the snow, and suddenly the simple act of movement takes over. No matter how significant the mountain is or how much care has gone into planning an expedition, there is a golden moment when a climber forgets what peak they are on, or how far they have to go, or how thirsty they are. The space in front of them is all that matters.

When they arrived at the base of their ridgeline, Lauren uncoiled the rope and Emmett clipped the rack to his harness and adjusted his helmet. They tried to drink some water and then pee before having to do so on a cliff, which would involve standing or squatting with a harness on as they leaned out from a belay stance. At seven or eight in the morning—no one remembers exactly when—they started up. They blew on their cold, bare hands, shaking them to keep blood flowing to their fingertips. The movement of climbing would warm them soon.

The first pitch was easy, but crumbling and wet. *Maybe the rock will clean up as we go*, Emmett thought to himself. After using as much of the rope as possible before its weight, running over the rock, tugged at him too much, Emmett built a belay, clipped himself to that with a locking carabiner, and put Lauren on belay. The rock was damp and cold. Small clumps of dirt, peppered with alpine wildflowers, sprouted from the ledge. Lauren followed Emmett up the pitch, and when she got to his belay she took the gear, arranged it on her harness, and cast out on the next pitch. The rock wasn't as bad here but it was interspersed with wet clumps of vegetation. "I called it bush pushing. Really vegetated. Low angle but really vegetated," Lauren says of the first few pitches.

After about twenty feet, Lauren turned back. She downclimbed back to Emmett's belay ledge. From here, she set off in another direction and this time she completed the pitch. But at this belay she told Emmett she wasn't interested in leading anymore; the dirty terrain and loose rock wigged her out.

"I don't feel comfortable with this," she said. "I think you'd better lead."

"You can lead higher up," Emmett offered. The rock looked better up there, sweeping toward the sky in cleaner, light-gray chunks. Lauren was the better technical climber; Emmett was more adventurous. If he could lead through the dirty stuff, he figured, she could take over when he got tired and when the rock better suited her strengths.

Emmett was enjoying himself. Their climb on this little peak wouldn't ever be an all-time classic. But this didn't temper the fact that he was climbing a new route in Alaska. After all the bushwhacking and work to get here, the climbing felt even more rewarding. For her part, Lauren remembers Emmett climbing better than she had ever seen him before. Though she was leery of continuing on lead, she was willing to trust her partner.

"As a second, she wasn't nervous," Emmett reasons. "She just seemed excited all day." He adds: "Maybe a little nervous leading in the crumbly stuff."

John and Alissa's ridgeline contained better rock quality for the most part. It was steeper, more sheer, and cleaner. Yet this was relative; John recalls how gingerly he and Alissa needed to move upward. "I don't think we were necessarily pulling chunks of rock off. What was there was pretty good. But on the ledges, there was a lot of loose blocks and stuff kicking around. It was really just scattered, with choss sitting around."

Like Lauren, Alissa felt uncomfortable leading after swapping a few pitches back and forth with John, so John led up throughout the day. Their ridgeline was a little harder. They stuck to clean rock if they could, and this meant staying on slabs or sheer cracks that were more devoid of holds. John tiptoed up in his stiff mountain-

eering boots, trusting the rubber to bite on little dime edges, applying downward pressure on the holds just so. He'd build a belay and
Alissa would follow, doing the same. At one point, they came to a
section that was memorable for how loose it was.

"That pitch was dangerous. There was no doubt. It was probably
a hundred feet or so with no pro because I didn't trust anything.
It wasn't hard climbing but it was just blocks scattered on blocks,
and they were big enough that you couldn't knock anything down
because Alissa was below me," John explains.

Pulling and pushing upward on *good* granite is delightful gym-
nastic movement. But on untrustworthy rock, weighting a foot or a
handhold turns into a nightmarish mental exercise. Pieces of pro-
tective gear such as cams and nuts are only as good as the medium
in which they're placed. Bad rock shears out, causing pieces to fail.
The most dangerous aspect is the risk of pulling something onto a
belayer or onto yourself. A follower can kick loose rock down, so
long as no other parties are below, but seconding a loose pitch is still
dangerous. A rope can get sliced on loose block or cut altogether.

Poor conditions like these aren't that common on most popular
roadside climbing destinations, because the rock cleans up the more
people climb on it. Of the four, John was the most experienced at
climbing choss. He'd spent the most time in alpine environments,
spots like the Canadian Rockies, where the mountains are cobbled-
together limestone. For Emmett, Alissa, and Lauren, the experience was newer. The longer climbs they had completed were better
traveled.

Soon, John and Alissa were higher on the peak than Emmett
and Lauren. Every once in a while, they heard their friends from the
other side of the ridge. They could make out the figures moving upward, and they grew slightly worried about the pace of their friends,
and whether or not Emmett and Lauren should keep going. "I think
we both had concerns. Not so much with the technical difficulty.

More so with the experience and the comfort level on that kind of terrain. Usually Lauren was typically the one that would try harder things. And she wasn't leading anything that day. Which put Emmett in the position of having to shoulder a lot of the responsibility," John says. "I think the difficulty of the climbing was within his ability. But I don't think he had a lot of experience with no-fall terrain. Or being in the mountains with bad rock."

"I was a little surprised that they were continuing up, at a certain point in the day," Alissa acknowledges.

As both teams got higher up on the mountain, rappelling the way they came made less and less sense because they'd lose more gear. They had two options for retreat: rappelling (either down the melting gully or down the jumbled, complicated ridges) or descending the gradual, easy backside of Sauron once they summited.

When climbers rappel, they thread the middle of the rope through an anchor—usually built from two or three pieces of gear—until both ends of the rope are down, able to be pulled through from below. With a sixty-meter rope threaded through an anchor and doubled over itself, a climber can rappel just thirty meters. Once down, a climber builds another anchor, waits for their partner to descend, and yanks the rope until it snakes down and the process is repeated. But there is no retrieving a rappel anchor. To save gear, climbers in the mountains get creative; slinging rope around big blocks of granite, drilling holes in the ice to thread a rope through. When they needed to descend, John, Alissa, Lauren, and Emmett could pool their resources, tie their two ropes together, and rappel sixty meters instead of thirty, and this was one of the reasons they'd chosen to climb on the same peak.

Rappelling is dangerous and climbers dread it even under good circumstances. A rope being pulled down can jam in a crack, a climber can slide off the ends of a rope accidentally, a rock can be dislodged yanking on a cord, and rappel anchors can fail. So the farther everyone got, the more committed they became to the climb: Each pitch would mean another long rappel on the way down, and this meant the safest and easiest option would be continuing up to the summit and then descending down the back side of the mountain, a meandering snowfield that would eventually lead them to their little base camp. Though no one knew for sure, all felt that climbing to the summit would be better than descending the way they came.

"It wasn't so tall that we thought we were going to have a problem summiting it in a day," John says, "but the rock quality was bad enough that it kept things slower than we would have liked, I think."

Though both teams were moving slower than they had anticipated, Emmett was climbing well. If Lauren or Emmett had concerns about continuing, they didn't voice them. For the first half of the day, the couple had climbed in the shade and they kept their boots on.

Emmett, leading, hoisted his body onto a small shelf on the ridge. He pasted the toe of his mountain boot against the rock, being careful not to move the angle of the rubber, and shifted his weight on it to be in line with his balance. He found a small crimp hold for his hand. The move was probably around the grade of 5.8 or 5.9. But the foothold gave way, and he caught himself, squeezing the handhold as his feet windmilled for a moment. His last piece of gear was about ten feet below him. He reeled himself back in, found his feet, lowered down. "I need to make sure I don't fall at all and I need to be really heads-up as I do my climbing to ensure that that doesn't happen," he remembers thinking. He needed to slow down, take it easy. This was the mountains—far from any help. You didn't fall in the mountains.

Emmett low down on the ridge.
*(Credit: Emmett Lyman Collection)*

Emmett and Lauren climbed another pitch in their rock boots. They poked out on the crest of the ridgeline and out of the shadow of the gully. Taking a minute, they removed their damp boots, being careful not to drop them. They clipped their boots to the anchor and let their bare feet dry out in the sun. They began to feel their soggy long underwear drying inside their softshell pants, windbreakers, and puffy coats. Emmett put on his rock shoes, which would afford more sensitivity than the clunky mountaineering boots.

Emmett and Lauren were having fun. If they were a little slower than their friends, that was okay. They could keep going at this pace. The terrain wasn't hard and they could just take their time through the loose sections and keep moving up.

Emmett climbed another pitch, following a crack that had good rock for forty feet or so.

Unlike much of the dirty climbing below, the moves here were engaging, enjoyable, and well protected. Climbing the crack is the last thing he remembers.

# PART II

# TEN

B y seven o'clock in the evening Emmett and Lauren were two-thirds of the way up Sauron. At the first belay station on the ridge they stopped to take a selfie with the mountains in the background. In the photograph, Lauren looks tired but happy; Emmett's scruff has grown more Alaskan by the hour. Both look like adventurers. They look like they are in love. It is the kind of photograph they'd send as a trip report for one of the climbing grants they'd gotten.

On the belay ledge, Lauren passed the rest of the equipment to Emmett, taking care not to drop anything. Emmett rearranged everything on his harness and then cast off up the next pitch, their sixth or seventh of the day.

Emmett climbed through grassy, hummocked ledges interspersed with blocks of granite. The terrain wasn't difficult here—around 5.8—and he wandered upward, placing a piece of gear every ten feet or so. From the small, sloping ledge of the belay, Lauren paid out rope, alternating between watching her partner and staring out at the expanse of Alaska. If she leaned her body against the angled rock, she could eke out a sitting position but couldn't sit down entirely. The day was spectacular—the best they'd had since setting up camp in the cirque. The dirty summertime snow ceded to the green valley beyond. A few wisps of clouds drifted high overhead, casting shadows and splotches of sunlight that glinted in the riverbed, miles below.

After what Lauren estimated to be fifty feet, Emmett traversed left over the other side of the ridge. For a moment, he climbed on the spine of the ridge itself, and then he crossed over and Lauren couldn't see him anymore. She could just hear him every once in a while. After about a hundred and fifty feet, nearly the end of a sixty-meter climbing rope, Emmett must have been looking for a spot to build a belay. Lauren would be able to climb up to him and they'd repeat the process four or five more times before reaching the summit. They were quite close to where they believed the terrain would ease up.

Then everything changed.

On her side of the ridge, Lauren heard the sound of Emmett falling: an audible, human cry mingled with the sound of rockfall tumbling down the mountain past her, a hundred feet to her left. She could not see Emmett and she had not seen the fall. The sound was massive, dust clouding the gully and sending snow and debris racing down.

Rock dust smells like cordite, the smokeless gunpowder once used in ammunition—granite smashing against granite. To Lauren, the snow cascading down after the rockfall looked like water as it slithered down the big gully.

"Somewhere in that moment the rope went tight," Lauren remembers. "Simultaneous to the thunder of rock I heard a human sound. It wasn't words. It was just a sound, maybe surprise and dismay. Which I figure was a sound that Emmett made as he was falling." When the rockfall subsided, Lauren realized she still had her hands clamped tight on the brake strand of the rope. With the friction of rope running against rock, it had not been difficult to catch the fall, and she did so instinctively.

Lauren remembers the quiet of the next moment because of how clear it was, how quickly everything around her returned to normal, back to uncaring, neutral mountains. "I think I was kind of shocked," she says. "I'm sure somewhere I knew exactly what had happened, but it took a second for my cognitive mind to add it all up."

She called out to him as the initial shock subsided.

*"Emmett! EMMETT!"* she yelled.

"There was an echo, so it made it hard to distinguish whether he was responding, but I was pretty sure that he wasn't." There was no tug on the rope. No response. "The longer I was calling to him the more frantic I started to feel." An obvious conclusion crept into her head: Emmett was probably dead. She didn't allow herself to think any further than that.

Lauren called for what felt like ten or fifteen minutes, though it was hard to tell; time lost all meaning. She began to think about what to do next. She still held Emmett's rope tight in her hand. Their bodies, with the rope running through Emmett's protection and Lauren's belay, acted like a counterweight to each other.

When humans encounter sudden trauma, the eyes and ears perceive stimuli first and send this information to the amygdala, the part of the brain that interprets and translates exterior stressors. During a traumatic or fear-filled event the amygdala kicks into overdrive as it's flooded with a substance called epinephrine: adrenaline. The surge in adrenaline allows the body to react quickly without thinking to, say, jump out of the way of oncoming traffic or grab a child who is about to fall off a playscape.

In these adrenaline-fueled moments, our brains trigger a fight, flight, or freeze response, a neurological holdover from our days as hunter-gatherers, when these lightning-fast reflexes allowed our ancestors to run, hide, or fight back based on a situation. The excess adrenaline allows us to react to an event that would otherwise be too overwhelming to deal with.

In his book, *Deep Survival*, a study of humans under stress, the journalist Laurence Gonzales explores the brain's relationship to traumatic situations. "Be aware that you're not all there," he writes. "You are in a profoundly altered state when it comes to perception, cognition, memory, and emotion." The brain, flooded with epinephrine, takes in information in a different way. "There is a new split, too, between cognition and emotion," he explains. "'Cognition' means reason and conscious thought. . . . 'Emotion' refers to a specific set of bodily changes in reaction to the environment. . . . Cognition is capable of making fine calculations and abstract distinctions. Emotion is capable of producing powerful physical actions."

In moments of extreme stress, we are governed by emotion, not cognition. This is a double-edged sword. "Most people," Gonzales continues, "are incapable of performing any but the simplest tasks under stress." People who operate in dangerous environments (firefighters, EMTs, mountain rescuers, pilots) train not because they will someday be able to avoid these emotional responses but rather so that they can rely on muscle memory when the stress hits.

Lauren's brain also had to process the additional fact that this was her life partner, the man she'd been with for three years. She could not flee, she could not fight, and she resisted the urge to freeze. Dealing with someone "who is injured or dead, especially someone you know, elicits powerful emotional changes," according to Gonzales.

Lauren remembers thinking about their dictum from base camp: *No falls.* They'd all agreed. No falls. She knew rock rescue, yet she had not been in a situation that resembled this. Few had. She grappled with her own instincts, but her brain was also making decisions as best it could. *Okay*, she thought. *I need to save my voice and save my energy.*

She needed to take some kind of direct action. First, she began tying off her belay device. Normally, this is accomplished by a single knot called a mule—the rock-climbing version of a trucker's hitch—that can be undone even under the load of a human's body weight. Lauren was good with knots and had always snatched up the mechanics of ropework quicker than most. But the cognitive side of her brain was working slowly. Instead of a mule knot, Lauren tied big overhand knots below her belay plate. While this imperfect solution would make the knots impossible to undo with Emmett's weight still on the rope, it allowed her to take her hands off the belay. She was too afraid to do anything else because further actions might move Emmett or lower him into the gully.

Both hands now free, she reached into her small climbing pack and pulled out the inReach. At 8:08 p.m., around ten minutes after Emmett fell, she texted Alissa and John.

"Helpemmett fell on lead. I can't see him and hes not responding to my calling."

HUNDREDS OF FEET ABOVE AND TO THE LEFT OF LAUREN AND EM-mett, John was wrestling with a 5.9 chimney pitch that was too wide to protect well with the cams they had with them. Pitches like this were John's forte. The scrappier it got, the better he seemed to do, as if he'd been built for cerebral, dangerous climbing, built to tackle the scary pitches where you needed to turn off those inward doubts and just roll up your sleeves.

John and Alissa's route had meandered up the left-hand ridgeline for the most part, but the climbing wasn't straightforward. Throughout the day, they'd woven around loose rock and gendarmes and ridges and scary flutings of old, rotten snow. They'd come for perfect rock in a pristine alpine setting and they'd gotten this: blue-collar climbing.

At least it sounded as if everyone was having fun—occasionally the two parties could hear each other, separated by the several hundred feet of mountain between the two routes. Earlier in the day, Alissa had traversed onto the right-hand side of the ridge just as Emmett had been taking a shit—he hadn't been able to go before climbing.

"Alissa! Go back over to your side of the ridge!" he'd admonished.

But Alissa was in the thick of it, trying to focus on the terrain and not fall. "I can't, Emmett!" she shouted.

Despite her tenuous position, it'd been hard for Alissa to not break out laughing. The situation was absurd. The moment had been one of the funny stories they'd eventually tell friends like Tom and Emily—though they'd probably leave it out of the official trip report.

By eight p.m., John and Alissa had climbed around nine or ten or eleven pitches; things blended together after twelve hours. Like Lauren and Emmett, they were moving slowly, taking their time with the loose blocks and bad rock, but they were about three hundred feet above and to the left of their friends, climbing toward the summit. At this point they were angling for a big shield of granite that loomed above them, the last true difficulty before they'd stand on top.

"It looked like that was clean rock," John tells me. "So we were kind of just going straight for that in hopes that it would be good rock. If not, we figured we could just keep going up similar terrain to what we were on."

As the day had worn on, the couple had worried over the slow pace of their friends, but this did not morph into alarm. Summiting first just meant they'd have to sit and wait on top before descending

John leading on the left ridgeline.
(Credit: Alissa Doherty)

together back to base camp. But the top of an unclimbed mountain in Alaska three days after the solstice wasn't a bad place to be. It was warm enough and there would be plenty of light.

"They're taking a long time over there," Alissa remembers thinking. But every once in a while, they could hear hoots and hollers, belay commands or the clanking of hexes or a happy voice, snatched by the wind and carried aloft toward them.

Neither Alissa nor John remembers hearing any rockfall. The day before, small stones and wet slides clattered down the peak in the rain throughout the day, but today had been utterly still, except for every once in a while, when the climbers would send down a loose block or two. But as John thrutched in the chimney, Alissa heard Lauren yelling. If John had heard anything, his brain had shut it out, focused on the moves in front of him, on what would keep him from falling. To Alissa the yells sounded repetitive and distinct. They didn't sound like the yells climbers made trying to communicate belay commands. Alissa shouted up to John.

"Do you hear that? I think it's Lauren."

"There's nothing I can do about it right now," John grunted from the chimney. He couldn't find a place for any gear; no matter how urgent it was, he still needed to climb to a better spot to build a belay.

With one hand, Alissa took the inReach out of her white pack, now clipped to the anchor, and belayed with the other. If John fell here, an inattentive belayer was the least of his worries.

"You okay? Heard Lauren shouting," she texted over the inReach.

At virtually the same time, her inReach made a little blip with the text from Lauren: "Helpemmett fell on lead."

"John!" Alissa yelled up. "Emmett's fallen!" The gravity of the situation needed few words to convey.

In order to reach Lauren and Emmett, John and Alissa would

have to cover unknown, difficult terrain, crossing into the gully that had been avalanching the day before and where the rockfall from Emmett's accident had cascaded down. Reaching Emmett would also mean having to leave much of their gear behind as they rappelled and traversed over to him. They had left base camp twelve hours ago. They were tired and dehydrated. While both were gripped by a fear common enough for rescuers—uncertainty at what they'd find—getting over to Emmett also meant putting themselves in unprecedented danger.

Moving sideways on a climb, or traversing, can be dangerous for both climbers on a rope team. Climbing normally, in a vertical, linear line, means the follower, belayed from above, can climb with a tight rope. But when a climbing team turns this process sideways, a leader risks swinging like a pendulum upon falling, as does the second climber.

More than dealing with the physical aspects of rappelling and traversing, though, there was concern about the type of terrain they'd have to cross. John and Alissa had stuck to the left-hand ridgeline because the ridgelines presented the safest lines to the summit. Neither had intended on entering the hollow, rotten stomach of the mountain. On either side of the gully lay a minefield of loose blocks and crumbling rock. The gradual slope was a low-angle nightmare, the kind of terrain that had slowed progress on Alissa's ascent of Liberty Ridge six years earlier. Anchors would be bad and hard to come by. Knocking something off, or being hit by something, or a rappel anchor failing—these were very real dangers.

John and Alissa were about to assume a risk they'd never anticipated or wanted. Despite this, neither hesitated for an instant. *It's your best friend,* John remembers thinking, as he kept thrashing up the chimney, climbing as fast as he could, trying to focus on the moves instead of the new situation they'd been thrown into. He belayed Alissa up to him. There were not many options available to them and there wasn't a lot of time. They would have to leverage caution against speed in order to save their friend.

First, they needed to get to a point on the mountain where they could see Emmett. Since the fall, no one had laid eyes on him. The climbing had led John and Alissa to the left of their ridge and around the corner, where they could see neither of their friends. If they regained the apex of the ridge, it would provide a clear vantage point to look down and to the right at both Emmett and Lauren.

"We are coming," Alissa typed back to Lauren. "Need to crest ridge then will rap to your side. Need 45 mins." Perhaps realizing how long those moments would seem, Alissa added a coda to her initial text. "Don't worry, we will get to him soon."

# ELEVEN

Alone on her sloping belay ledge three hundred feet below, it dawned on Lauren what her friends were attempting and she began to worry that John and Alissa would be killed or hurt in the process. From what Lauren could see of the terrain above and to the left of her, their plan appeared impossible and dangerous. The rock was a mess. If John and Alissa approached from above, they'd likely dislodge more loose rock. It could fall onto Emmett, or onto her.

"Alissa had messaged me and said they were planning to rap in to Emmett. And I remember thinking, Well, gosh, I don't know," Lauren says. "I think they were just gonna go do it. And I guess if I was in their position, it would have been very hard to say no."

Lauren realized that she would be on her ledge for a long time. *Okay. We're going to be here for a bit*, she remembers thinking. The cognitive side of her brain was taking over, adding everything up and calculating what would need to be done. All three needed to live; their survival was the only way Emmett was getting off the mountain. The worst thing that could happen now was for some accident to create more victims. She focused on staying calm and not allowing her brain to travel to the dark corners it wanted to.

"I had all these things that were running through my mind. But that's where this new gear just kicks in. I can totally remember all these thoughts, but your mind just goes . . . *Whoop, we're gonna shut that one down.* You start running in this direction and another fire door goes down."

Lauren took off her rock shoes and put her boots back on. She reached into her backpack to pile on the rest of her warm layers. She had nothing in the way of bivouac gear, little for warm clothes, and her ledge was losing the sunlight she and Emmett had basked in earlier. Camp was still visible, and the survival blanket and the oxycodone and the first aid kit were tucked away among their supplies down there. The tents represented an oasis of safety in the sudden, oppressive loneliness of the place.

After twenty or thirty minutes, Lauren felt distinct tugs on the rope. Emmett was still alive. "Presumably, that was him regaining consciousness," she reflects. "I think that's when I resumed calling his name. And . . . at that point it sounded like he was making a sound in response. It was quite weak and it didn't sound like he was saying words. It was still kind of hard to distinguish: Is this an echo or what?

"I was calling his name, but once I heard him making a sound I asked, 'Are you okay? What do you need?' I found I'd get no sound in response to these types of questions. It was only when I said 'Emmett' that there would be some response."

Emergency medical personnel assess a patient's level of consciousness using a standardized scale with the acronym AVPU: alert, verbal, pain, unresponsive. A fully conscious patient is alert and oriented to their surroundings. As a patient's level of consciousness decreases, they may only be responsive to verbal or painful stimuli. If they deteriorate further, they are unresponsive: the bottom end of the scale. Emmett *was* responsive to verbal stimuli, but Lauren was relatively certain he was not fully alert.

When a human is hit as hard in the head as we must assume Emmett was, the body goes into survival mode. Blood rushes to protect vital organs, and the brain and heart are the most important of these organs. The pulse slows down, while blood pressure increases to allow for a greater volume of blood into the cranium— essentially sending every available resource to the brain. Patients with a traumatic brain injury (TBI) eventually exhibit specific, alarming signs of trauma. Dark patches called raccoon eyes grow around their eyes. And patterned bruising called Battle's sign occurs behind a person's ears. These specific marks indicate a patient has a skull fracture and that blood is pooling between the skull and the brain cavity. People who survive the initial trauma are often afflicted with severe neurological changes that affect personality and brain function.

No one had reached Emmett, so all this was speculative. His responses provided the only metric to gauge the severity of his injuries, and he only responded to his name. But Emmett responding was better than Emmett *not* responding. He was alive. And because Lauren was positive she could hear his voice, sent in scattered scraps around to her side of the ridge, she was feeling more optimistic.

At 8:52, Lauren texted Alissa and John again. "I think he might be talking."

"OK Good. We are going as quickly as we can."

"No SOS yet. Should I call? Global rescue."

In hindsight, it may be easy to wonder why Lauren didn't do more in those early moments. Why hadn't she immediately pressed the SOS button to call for help? Why hadn't she ascended to Emmett to check on him? Such a maneuver was possible, even if it was dangerous considering the loose terrain.

But in reality, her options were limited. She had trained in rock rescue, the specific art of escaping a belay and lowering a victim, and her climbing partners all attest to Lauren's knowledge. But these maneuvers assume a victim is close to civilization and has somewhere to go, not that a rescuer is alone in an area inaccessible by road.

Lauren *did* consider tying Prusik slings—cords wrapped around a hanging rope like a Chinese finger trap that allow a climber to ascend—and trying to get to Emmett, but she was terrified the climbing rope had been cut partway through and that the back-and-forth sawing motion that comes with ascending a rope might sever it completely. She also couldn't lower Emmett: He'd used up too much rope on his lead and he was so far to her left that to lower him would simply send him into the gully. But her main concern was that the gully itself was dangerous. If it *had* been a spontaneous rockfall that had knocked Emmett off the wall, would more follow?

When rock rescue is taught in American Mountain Guides Association courses, even the practice drills assume a patient has suffered a comparatively benign injury, such as a cracked ankle, and that a rescue would occur in a similarly friendly environment: a place with bolted rappel stations or other modern cliff-side amenities. For instructors and students alike, the implicit understanding is that, in more extreme scenarios, self-rescue is not possible.

In 2010, the professional climber Steve House, then regarded as the best alpinist in the United States, fell when a foothold broke away from the crumbling limestone on the north face of Mount Temple in the Canadian Rockies, above the resort town of Lake Louise. House fell eighty feet. He felt several pieces of gear ping out of the rock as he was airborne before he slammed onto a ledge.

In his autobiography, *Beyond the Mountain*, House recalls: "I hurt like I have never hurt before. I remember telling Bruce [Miller, House's partner] to get out the cell phone to call for help. He did not yet know how bad it was. I knew." House had broken his pelvis in two different places, had seven small fractures in his spine, and had fractured six ribs. For an agonizing half hour, House crawled back on a broad horizontal shelf toward Miller's belay before a Parks Canada helicopter flew in to rescue them.

Like Jim Sweeney, the climber who fell in the Elevator Shaft on Mount Johnson in 1989, you couldn't call House's injuries minor by any stretch. But each were, at least, partially aware of their predicament.

"To bring somebody down who is impaired in any way, but who is as impaired as Emmett, would have been suicidal," Lauren says, speaking of trying to get Emmett down without John and Alissa through the jumbled terrain they'd climbed up all day. "And he wouldn't have made it. He would have died in the course of that."

Beyond the physical problems of rescuing Emmett, some part of Lauren may have recognized she wasn't able to fully be herself in this moment, and that her emotional closeness to Emmett was in no small way impacting her judgment. Emmett wasn't just a climbing partner—he was the man she loved, too. Lauren waited for her friends and tried to keep herself as calm as possible. Emmett's salvation—and her own—now rested in part with the fact that John and Alissa were climbing over to them, that they'd chosen to climb on the same peak. Still, all three knew what the outcome might be. If Emmett was as injured as they suspected, they were climbing now out of a desire to make sure Emmett at least had somebody there with him when he died.

AFTER JOHN BUILT A BELAY AND BROUGHT ALISSA UP TO HIM through the chimney pitch, he was able to traverse right for a hundred feet. From his new vantage point he could see Lauren at her belay. He could also see Emmett, who was indeed moving, and this was a great relief. The two were about three hundred feet below John and Alissa.

When John yelled to Emmett he responded, but he wasn't making any sense. Even from a distance, Emmett looked awful. His orange, lightweight Styrofoam climbing helmet had been blown off by the impact. "We noticed his motions were weird. He was obsessed with getting his harness off. He'd keep pushing his harness with his hands," John remembers. But he was alive.

Looking up, Lauren could also see John. He gave her a little wave. The sight of her friend injected a new hope. *They were coming. They were really coming for them.*

At this point, neither Alissa nor Lauren had yet called for a rescue, though it had been an hour since Emmett's fall—an hour that had both flown past and moved painfully slowly. In part, this was because all three had been initially preoccupied with tasks that felt more urgent. There was also still uncertainty about how Emmett was doing. And everyone's brains were doing funny things after the accident. "You see less, hear less, miss more cues from the environment, and make mistakes," Gonzales writes of the brain under stress. But after the first hour there was little doubt: If Emmett were to live, they'd need outside help.

Marc Chauvin, a past president of the American Mountain Guides Association as well as one of the first American guides to work in Europe, notes a distinct difference in how Americans perceive rescue and how it's carried out across the Atlantic. He's not sure the shift toward communication devices and the increased pressure it puts on rescuers is such a bad thing—far from it, in fact. "Europeans don't see rescue as separate from their decision-making. They see it as *part* of their trip planning," he tells me. Until recently, this wasn't true in the United States, where the marrow of self-reliance is also used to sell jackets and first aid kits at REI: *Buy this, and you can survive anything.* Americans tend to view heading into the wilderness as a method of gaining independence, and this DIY attitude leaves little psychological wiggle room to call for help.

"I've never met anyone with a broken leg who was self-reliant," Chauvin says and shrugs. "The average person who does this recreationally has been sold a bill of goods: Accidents only happen to foolish people."

"When climbers get to talking about risk, the subject of self-rescue versus calling for a rescue tends to come up and with some predictability self-rescue is very much valued and calling for rescue seems to be seen as weak and irresponsible," Lauren tells me. "To acknowledge that you cannot on your own get out of the situation you find yourself in is a vulnerable thing. . . . But it is not black and white: self-rescue or get rescued. It is a continuum. Plenty of climbing accidents have circumstances that allow for self-rescue. Others do not. We need to be knowledgeable enough to assess. That's part of the preparation."

Lauren's typed-out rescue plan, the ten-page pdf she'd written in the months before the trip, had outlined specific plans for various situations. All the climbers had agreed on these. In the document, she had coded injuries or other possible situations like a traffic stoplight: red, yellow, and green. In a code-red scenario, a team member would send a direct message to Global Rescue.

At 9:04 p.m., Alissa texted Lauren. "Have you heard him talk again? John said he looked up when he called him."

At 9:08, an hour after Emmett fell, Lauren sent out a text to Global Rescue. "Emergency my partner fell rock climbing he is conscious but injured please help."

# TWELVE

In Chamonix, France, or Banff, Canada, members of elite mountain rescue squadrons remain on standby to save hikers or injured climbers, tasked with performing rescues on a near-daily basis. In France, outdoor enthusiasts head into the mountains content in the knowledge that, when a climb becomes too dangerous to continue or a partner falls or breaks an ankle on the descent, a B3 helicopter and a few elite rescuers will snatch an injured climber off their perch and whisk them back down to town. In many instances, these rescues are free of charge.

Mountaineering has been enmeshed in European culture for hundreds of years, and Chamonix is heralded as the sport's capital. The region's Mont Blanc massif is compact and well traveled; the line between mountain and infrastructure is blurry—trams and lifts shuttle skiers and climbers from valley to peak and back again with ease. The elite PGHM—Peloton de Gendarmerie de Haute Montagne—is a branch of specialized mountain police funded by the French government for good reason: In the Mont Blanc massif, an average of one hundred mountain sports enthusiasts die per year and countless others need rescuing. The culture is such that alpinists jockey for space on the cover of *Paris Match* alongside television stars and singers. The popularity of mountaineering and the concentration of climbing accidents, along with those from skiing and hiking, leads to government funding for rescue personnel, which leads to equipment and training, and this gets results.

In contrast, the popularity of mountaineering in the United States is relatively new, and the growing population who practice it do so in an assortment of different locations: private land, national parks, state parks, and everything in between. And, barring a few notable exceptions, most areas in the United States lack highly trained mountain rescue teams.

National parks see the most support, and in several of those parks, the search and rescue job is orchestrated by climbing rangers: crack mountaineers with decent résumés. But these few climbing rangers contend with threadbare budgets. In Denali National Park, a few helicopter pilots remain on standby within the park's bounds, which is a rarity. Yosemite's climbing rangers (there are two) are supported by YOSAR (Yosemite Search and Rescue), a cadre of dedicated climbers who wear their meager living conditions and wages as a badge of honor. They are not paid until a rescue occurs, at which point they become park service employees. Most YOSAR members are top climbers themselves, and they, along with climbing rangers in the Tetons and Denali, have a helicopter to use at all times. A few other national parks with a heavy flow of climbing traffic—such as Rainier and Rocky Mountain in Colorado—have staffed climbing rangers. But the positions are seasonal, and the employees are at the mercy of budget cuts as the winds blow back and forth in Washington, DC.

Much of the rescue work outside of national parks—a sizable portion—is completed by volunteers or entities like the National Guard. In a January 2020 article in *Outside* with the ominous title

"America's Search and Rescue Is in a State of Emergency," correspondent Marc Peruzzi noted that American search and rescue (SAR) operations "are a patchwork. Depending on where you are when bad luck strikes, you might be saved by a commando squad with a chopper on speed dial . . . or forced to wait hours, even days, until well-meaning volunteers with limited resources reach you in the backcountry."

In my mid-twenties, when I made a threadbare living as a mountain guide, I began volunteering with New Hampshire's Mountain Rescue Service (MRS), one of the ad hoc volunteer groups that fill in the gaps of climbing support in the United States. The spirited, New England town-hall ethos of the team makes rescues and trainings feel like a Norman Rockwell painting with GORE-TEX. At a typical board meeting, North Face–sponsored athletes and Carhartt-wearing homesteaders banter about which static ropes and radios to spend the team's sparse budget on.

MRS's forty volunteers vary in age, from aspiring guides in their mid-twenties with plenty of legs and lungs under them to grizzled team members who have been on board since the team's inception in 1971. Half the time, MRS callouts are fun, for lack of a better word: Usually a hiker is lost or has some benign injury such as a sprained ankle.

For alpinists looking to prepare for uncertainty, the surprise jangle of the phone in a pocket at five o'clock (the hour most people realize they've bitten off more than they can chew) is free training: Navigating through dense New England drainages or stumbling around in sixty-mile-per-hour wind at midnight after guiding all day is the kind of mental and physical beatdown mountaineers relish. At best, a rescue is a way to catch up with old friends and responders from all different age groups and political spectrums—volunteerism at its finest.

Usually, injured or lost hikers call for help with little inkling of what a rescue entails. Most Americans probably envision a helicopter whirring above their location after fifteen or twenty minutes. But, as Peruzzi points out, help might be hours—or days—away. In New Hampshire, for instance, a phone call is relayed through a 911 dispatcher to the US Forest Service or New Hampshire Fish and Game. If the weather is nasty enough or the snow conditions dangerous enough that these entities need outside help, they call MRS. It takes time for a volunteer team to organize, pack, and drive to a trailhead or cliff. Hiking and searching takes several more hours. If a victim is injured, carrying them out in a litter takes upward of twelve hours, so rescuers will try anything to make a victim walk.

This system (the "find, make walk" system, for lack of a better term) is archaic but it works, and there's been little pressure (or available funding) to fix it. Chances are, if you call for help in the woods in the United States, a volunteer group like MRS will be the one who comes after you. Chances are, too, they'll arrive far later than you want them to.

The more complicated task of rescuing injured climbers from technical terrain is more serious but not uncommon. And yet, during the typical eight-day Wilderness First Responder (WFR) course, which is a prerequisite for being on most SAR teams in the United States, most classroom time is spent going over blisters, poison ivy treatment, and icing sprained ankles in the backcountry. The grisly bread and butter of climbing falls—sucking chest wounds, severe hypothermia, torn aortas, broken femurs and pelvises, and traumatic brain injuries—are usually skipped over. This makes sense; the course is geared toward wilderness therapy instructors tasked with minding delinquent teenagers, not rescuers responding to a grave injury. When these bad scenarios occur, it's unlikely most treatment in the field, away from a hospital, would be helpful. In these instances there's little course of action apart from immediate evacuation.

The notion of self-rescuing someone in Emmett's position, or of administering any kind of care that would make a difference, is a pipe dream. Climbers are either okay, dead, or dying. If they fall into the dying category, only immediate evacuation can save them.

# THIRTEEN

When Lauren sent her text at 9:08 p.m., it traveled five thousand miles and several time zones and was received by a dispatcher working for Global Rescue.

Along with the text, the dispatcher received the GPS coordinates from the inReach device, and these they forwarded to the Alaska state troopers. Though technically the state troopers have jurisdiction over rescues, other organizations are often called in. The National Park Service runs its own operation within Denali National Park, where the majority of climbers tend to head in Alaska. If either of these entities needs help, though, they'll call the Alaska Rescue Coordination Center (AKRCC), which is housed at Joint Base Elmendorf-Richardson, a sprawling complex outside Anchorage that contains the people power and machinery—and expertise—to rescue anyone in Alaska. The AKRCC, run by the federal government, coordinates with multiple agencies to "provide 24-hour rescue coordination capability in support of US military and civil aviation search and rescue (SAR) needs in the Alaska search and rescue region (SRR)." This means monitoring radio frequencies and assisting any entity, such as the National Park Service or state troopers, who need it.

To achieve this, the AKRCC coordinates with the 176th Wing of the Alaska Air National Guard, also housed at Elmendorf. Alaska is the biggest state in the union, and with size comes variety. The squadrons of the 176th are tasked with an oddball assortment of jobs, both in Alaska and abroad. The same guardsman may be called to, say, airlift the abandoned bus that Chris McCandless, the famous protagonist of *Into the Wild*, lived in for the final two months of his life, or to rescue Saudi fighter pilots who have ditched their F-15 in the Red Sea. Personnel rotate between missions overseas and providing civilian search and rescue in Alaska, operating under the notion that little can provide better training for overseas combat and civilian missions than the state's varied, taxing terrain and weather.

The 176th Wing is comprised of three separate squadrons: the 210th, 211th, and 212th. The 210th operates an HH-60 Pave Hawk, a modified version of the Sikorsky Black Hawk helicopter outfitted for both combat and civilian search and rescue. The Pave Hawk's main difference from its more famous counterpart lies in the form of a massive refueling probe that protrudes from the helicopter's front end, giving a midflight Pave Hawk the profile of a gigantic mosquito.

The 211th rescue squadron, meanwhile, flies an HC-130 Hercules, a variant of the classic Lockheed Martin C-130 military transport plane, which, in one form or another, has flown American military personnel for more than sixty years. A Hercules provides long-range support to the Pave Hawk helicopter. This means being able to refuel the Pave Hawk in midair, by way of two massive hoses that deploy off the external fuel tanks on either side of the wings of the Hercules. The increased fuel capacity allows the aircraft to fly in remote areas without having to land to refuel. A Pave Hawk's long-range capability is greater than a Black Hawk's, as much of the space in the rear cabin is taken up by an auxiliary fuel tank.

In addition to the flight crews, each aircraft flies out of Elmendorf with pararescuemen from the 212th squadron on board. PJs (pararescue jumpers) are the most storied rescuers in the United States: equal parts commando and first responder, accustomed to dropping into dangerous war zones and mountain terrain alike. The 212th PJ unit that operates out of Elmendorf is the busiest in the country.

In order to become a PJ, an applicant must pass a grueling series of training and physical tests. "The pipeline," as it's known, lasts upward of two years or so, depending on how well a trainee's body holds up to the battering it receives. Only twenty percent of would-be PJs withstand the abuse, an attrition rate higher than BUD/S, the training program for Navy SEALs.

Trainees must master a decathlon of skills in order to pass muster: survival behind enemy lines, rescue swimming, and rock and ice climbing, to name a few. You've got to be able to administer an IV in a helicopter that's being shot at, or fire off fifty push-ups in two minutes. "Of all the skills that are required in this profession, none are more important than the others. You never know where you're going to get called to that day," PJ Dave Shuman told a podcaster in 2016. In a typical training exercise, two trainees are forced to share a snorkel, remaining underwater while an instructor batters their heads each time they break the surface. They're buckled into the fuselage of a Pave Hawk, dunked underwater, and forced to escape. They load their rucksacks and jog up mountain passes. It's not unheard of for a death to occur in the pipeline.

If alpinists need to be fit, PJs need to be indestructible. The job is taxing and dangerous, so it makes sense that the pipeline is, too. "Many pararescue operators have been killed during training, but that level of training is necessary to prepare for the worst-case scenarios inherent in the job," Jimmy Settle writes in his book *Never Quit* about preparing for the 212th.

The culmination of the pipeline is an event called "hell night," which allows the instructors as much masochistic wiggle room as the name implies. ("It's a surprise and a complete mindfuck," Settle writes.) Aspiring PJs are doused with fire hoses, drowned in the pool, forced to hump heavy logs in perverse tandem with one another, and ordered to complete round after round of flutter kicks and push-ups until the lactic acid forces them to quit or drop to the ground or both.

Pararescuers excel at saving lives in remote places. They train as paramedics, though many are physicians assistants. They ride onboard ambulances in high-crime areas before deploying in order to become accustomed to gunshot wounds and other severe trauma. Overseas, PJs have to evacuate injured servicepeople as well as civilians, and they often take on combat duties while on rescues.

"When the pilots go down at sea, the PJs, as they're known, jump with scuba gear. When they go down on glaciers, they jump with crampons and ice axes. When they go down in the jungles, they jump with two hundred feet of tree-rappelling line. There is, literally, nowhere on earth a PJ can't go," Sebastian Junger writes in *The Perfect Storm*.

And no other PJ squadron gets more civilian search and rescue operations than the 212th. Along with the 210th and the 211th, it is responsible for saving civilian lives in Alaska: hikers or hunters or Denali climbers or downed light-aircraft pilots. You name it, they've saved it.

"They call Alaska PJ heaven," one of them tells me.

AT 9:14, SIX MINUTES AFTER LAUREN TEXTED GLOBAL RESCUE, TONY Bannock, an office employee of Regal Air, the charter service that had flown the four climbers to Tired Pup Creek on the 17th, decided to check in on the four climbers more or less on a whim. He'd not heard from them for a little while after they left Anchorage.

"Welfare check. All good?" he messaged Alissa.

It was not. When Alissa got the note, she and John were in the thick of rappelling, and she did not respond until forty minutes later.

"Hey Tony, about two hours ago, one of our climbers took a serious fall. We have contacted Global Rescue and they are working on getting help. We are in the midst of reaching him. The terrain is highly technical so it will be a few hours before we can reach him and can assess."

"Do you need heli support? Want me to contact troopers? Text my friend Keenan in the rescue coordination center in the air guard," Tony texted back. By chance, or perhaps by the nature of Anchorage's tight-knit community, Bannock was close friends with Keenan Zerkel, who had just taken the helm at the AKRCC.

Luck, as the Roman philosopher Seneca put it, is when preparation meets opportunity. And this small, personal connection between the climbers and the head of the busiest rescue command center in the United States was a piece of serendipity. Being able to text Zerkel directly might have seemed like a little fortunate blip in an otherwise unlucky day, but this piece of happenstance meant that the 176th Wing was put on alert sooner than they might have been otherwise. Zerkel's awareness of the situation probably shaved hours of logistics off the response time.

By around 10:00 p.m.—two hours after Emmett's accident and just forty-five minutes after Lauren had texted Global Rescue—members of the 176th Wing began getting ready. Phones started buzzing. In one of her texts to Global Rescue, Lauren had outlined what she suspected Emmett's injuries were: "head injury, maybe broken bones or internal." She had also described the loose nature of the terrain she and the rest of the team were in. These details, as well as the coordinates from the inReach, were what the AKRCC had to go on.

Corey Ercolani, one of the crew assigned to the Pave Hawk that night, had just put his daughter to sleep. Like many in the 210th, Ercolani lived in Anchorage full-time. A Pennsylvania native, he'd been doing combat and rescue operations in Alaska and overseas for thirteen years. Ercolani had joined the military to pay for college, but after 9/11, he wanted to pursue a career in the armed forces that would make a real difference. He headed to Alaska.

"I just consolidated and sold everything, packed a small truck full of my belongings, and drove up to Alaska and showed up on the door of the squadron," Ercolani tells me. Soon thereafter, he began working as a full-time guardsman on a Pave Hawk. A standard Pave Hawk crew consists of four guardsmen: pilot, copilot, and two what are now called special mission aviators, though the designation has changed throughout the years. At the time, Ercolani's position was titled flight engineer, and he ran the helicopter's takeoff and landing data. He also ran the hoist, the 180-foot steel cable that dangled from the cabin and was used for extraction. A fellow special mission aviator, Anthony Guedea, would also ride in the cabin, along with a PJ and the combat rescue officer (CRO) whose job it would be to coordinate the rescue.

Chris Keen, the CRO on duty that night, was at home, too, and he hopped in his truck and drove the short distance to Elmendorf. Keen had been a PJ before becoming a CRO, so he was, like his counterparts, well versed in saving lives in scary places.

When Keen got to Elmendorf, he met with the on-duty PJ, Willis Strouse. Neither knew what to expect, but they were used to that. A climber had fallen, he was badly hurt, and he was in the middle of nowhere. Bringing on additional help might not be a bad idea. Strouse tracked down an off-duty PJ, Staff Sargeant Adam Brister, who was getting ready to go to bed after grabbing dinner in town.

"We need an extra hand," Brister remembers being told. "Get your stuff."

Brister, a friendly Louisianan, is a more or less typical PJ. He's built like a football player, which he was, but he balances that with genuine compassion sometimes missing in other branches of the special forces. When I first spoke with him, he was adamant that the rescues he performs are nothing special—that he's just one of a bunch of people doing this. And in a way, he's right. PJs do stuff all the time that seems crazy to an onlooker. I also got the sense he was protecting himself from the ribbing he expects will come from talking about yourself to a writer. Humility—the notion of just putting your head down and getting the job done—is important in this field.

Brister had gone to college on a football scholarship and bounced around with a few odd jobs afterward. On the verge of accepting an officer commission with the army, he visited his uncle, a retired PJ. The job sounded like a fantasy. Jumping out of planes and helicopters into oceans and mountains to save people's lives?

"I saw the light, as they say. The next day I went to the air force recruiter and said, 'I want to be a PJ.'" And if you were a PJ, you might as well head up to Alaska. "When you're on alert you're doing three to four missions a *week* during the busy season," Brister says.

The men grabbed everything they assumed they'd need from prepackaged duffel bags. For his part, Brister, and probably many of the others as well, thought the mission would be a simple hoist operation—winch down to a glacier to help some mountaineer—and that it wouldn't take too long. You couldn't bring everything, and in the melee, Brister didn't grab the duffel bag with his snow-shoes and warm clothing.

Soon everyone was throwing gear into a few trucks and head-ing toward the flight line, where the Pave Hawk and the Hercules were fueling up and getting ready. Two additional PJs boarded the Hercules with extra equipment. The two aircraft had more gear than an REI, ready to rescue anyone in the state.

The Pave Hawk was piloted by Dave Breun, an aircraft commander who only had a few months to go before retiring after seventeen years of flying with the Air National Guard. He was about as experienced as anyone could get in this line of work.

Still, the Hidden Mountains were an unknown entity. And while yes, the 176th performed technical climbing rescues, it wasn't their prime discipline. They were polymaths, not specialists. Plus, getting to Emmett before he died was as much about the condition of the weather as the caliber of the men. But with a single text, Lauren had unleashed millions of dollars of training, manpower, and expertise, and all this was now on the verge of barreling toward the coordinates that had, until yesterday, been nothing more than another random, desolate spot in a state brimming with them.

For hikers or hunters or climbers without some kind of communication device, alerting the AKRCC isn't an option. When climbers kept their satellite phones in base camp, the chances of getting plucked off a ledge were far slimmer than they are now. Alpinists used to be on their own. Now, for better or worse, they're not. "We have so much more connectivity now," says Madaleine Sorkin, a Coloradan who juggles being one of the finest big-wall climbers in the United States with spearheading an initiative called the Climbing Grief Fund, an organization that deals with traumatic incidents in the mountains. "Our reality has totally shifted."

At 11:51 p.m., Global Rescue sent a text to Lauren. The rescue team would launch in ten minutes.

The weather in Anchorage was perfect. People all over the city still lapped up the warm, perpetual light of solstice in Alaska, as the crew prepared for departure.

The second the flight crews and PJs left the ground, they would be assuming responsibility for the life of a complete stranger. With his injuries, Emmett wouldn't make it through the night. If anyone had a chance of saving him, it was these men. The Pave Hawk and the HC-130 took off. The sounds of rotors and propellers joined the whine of aircraft aloft over summertime Anchorage, and they headed west toward the Hidden Mountains.

# FOURTEEN

At 9:52 p.m., around the time Brister had been finishing dinner, John and Alissa rigged their first rappel to try and get to Emmett from the point they'd climbed to on the left-hand ridge. The couple faced a practical conundrum: Every time they doubled their sixty-meter rope to lower themselves, they left two or three pieces of gear behind that they'd never be able to get back, abandoned as a rappel anchor. They only had one rope and could rappel only one hundred feet at a time, so this meant leaving a lot of gear. Each time they went down, their small rack of cams and nuts got smaller still. They counted on reaching Emmett and then being able to use the gear he had on his harness.

From where they were, traversing hard right in order to reach a direct line *above* Emmett was impossible—the terrain petered off and no obvious way of traversing presented itself. This left the gully they'd all taken care to avoid earlier. Neither party had considered heading into the gully in the first place and to do so now seemed dangerous. It cut deeply between the two ridgelines and they couldn't see anywhere that would allow access to Emmett and Lauren. Directly to their right was the widest part of the gully, which John and Alissa hoped to avoid because of the wet slides they'd witnessed the day before. Instead they rappelled, angling right and toward a narrower and rockier part of the gully, hoping each time they pulled the rope and abandoned more gear above them that they'd be able to start climbing across instead of going down. The nighttime air was chilly and damp and progress was very slow. The physical and practical difficulty of getting to Emmett's ridge consumed them and they pushed their thirst and tiredness out of their minds. Like Lauren, neither had the psychological bandwidth to think beyond the simple, mechanical act of climbing.

"I think you flip on a rescue switch," John says. "We would have done that even if it was a stranger. We were shouting to him the whole time, reassuring him that we were coming, in case he was conscious enough to be afraid we'd left him."

Four years earlier, Alissa had been climbing at a small outcrop of cliff called Ragged Mountain in Connecticut when Sam Streibert fell from a popular easy climb and hit the ground from about thirty feet up. Streibert was a legendary figure in the East Coast climbing community. A pioneer of many of the area's classic routes, he'd been putting up new climbs since the 1960s. But that day, Streibert's foot slipped and he fell. His second piece of gear popped out of the rock and he hit the ground. Alissa, right next to Streibert, saw and heard the whole thing.

The sound of a falling climber—the jangle of gear, of sudden surprise—is sickening. Alissa, the first person to reach Streibert, remembers freezing for ten seconds before rushing over to him, afraid she was about to witness a man die. Later, these ten seconds of hesitation haunted her, even though, after an airlift to Hartford, Streibert ended up recovering. "I felt like I hadn't done a good enough job," Alissa remembers. "I think now, whenever I see an accident, I go there and try to compensate for the fact that I felt like I didn't do a great job with Sam."

After five or so rappels with their single sixty-meter rope, they had angled into the gully itself, which, at their elevation, split into two smaller chimneys: gashes in the middle of the mountain that cut so deeply on either side they were hard to escape from. By now, the rock was oozing with moisture; the temperatures hovered just above freezing. A cold fog blew in and further soaked everything. John rappelled first, sliding down the ropes, letting his climbing boots sink into soft snow. Everything was wet. He fed out some slack in the ropes so he could cross over, still on rappel, to the right-hand side of the gully. He found the most protected place he could, built an anchor. Somewhere to their right lay Emmett. They still hadn't found a feasible way to traverse out of the narrow gully and over to him, so they planned on making another rappel down the gully in the hopes they could climb right and reach Lauren. From there, they'd be able to reclimb Emmett's pitch to get to him.

"Alissa!" John yelled up. "Off rappel!"

Alissa fed the two strands of rope through her belay device, checked them, leaned back, and lowered herself into the gully until she reached John. The stance they'd been edged into was dripping with water, but it was the only place they had been able to find to build an anchor. They pulled on one end of the rope and the red cord slid down and snaked in messy coils in the slushy snow. They threaded the ends of the rope again, this time through their new anchor, and John put his belay device back on the rope. He repeated the process, rappelled another hundred feet, and was searching for his next anchor when Alissa saw something the size of a microwave slam into the gully just a few feet from her stance. It was a rock, and Alissa noticed it was covered in blood. "For a second I thought it had just hit me in the head." She put her hand up to her face, then up to her helmet. Then it dawned on her it was Emmett's blood—not hers—that was smeared all over the boulder. "Emmett was directly above me. And he had knocked it off, I guess because he was flailing up there."

She screamed up: "Don't move, Emmett! Don't move!"

Then she threaded the ropes and made the next rappel to John.

By now it was around midnight and Alissa and John were just a pitch away from Lauren. Both were exhausted and stressed, beyond thinking about mistakes. Each climber must have been moving into that realm of trancelike motion, of praying nothing will go wrong, of hoping against hope everything will work out, of being powerless to do otherwise. The terrain between them and Lauren, a 5.7 slab traverse out of the gully, would normally have been easy for both, who were 5.12 climbers. But the traverse was sopping wet and John couldn't see any place to put in what little gear he had left. There was also no choice but to keep going, so he put his head down and tried not to think about any of this and just started climbing. Alissa belayed as though holding the rope would keep John from hurting himself if he fell. She sat still, getting soaked to the bone at her stance. John kept going, pasting his shoes to the damp, grimy rock, trying not to fall, trying to climb as fast as he could.

AT AROUND ONE IN THE MORNING ON JUNE 24TH, FIVE HOURS AF-ter Emmett had fallen, and four since Lauren had texted Global Rescue, Dave Breun and his copilot, Seth Peterson, poked the nose of the Pave Hawk into the small pass that marked the entrance to the cirque. "When we were first flying in, the weather was great," Adam Brister remembers. "But as soon as we got to the Neacolas the cloud cover was so low and it was like we were flying through soup it was so foggy." For the past hour, they'd taken a circuitous route through the Hidden and Neacola Mountains, weaving around the peaks to deal with the weather. A low cloud bank was settling into the range, and the Pave Hawk whipped through it as it flew west.

Far above them, the HC-130 flew circles around the area, waiting to refuel the helicopter.

The cloud bank hovered at an elevation of about five thousand feet, which was around five hundred feet below where Emmett lay stranded on a ledge, but the rescuers could see the climbers' base camp, which was perched just below at an elevation of around forty-five hundred feet. These tents *had* to be the climbers who had called for help. Who else would be out here?

Though no one could see the mountains in real life, Corey Ercolani, the flight engineer, stared at the topography beyond the veil of clouds on his monitor. The mountains around them were steep and complicated. This wasn't going to be a simple hoist. "On a civilian airliner," Ercolani explains, "they just have a heading and air speed and they climb to an altitude and they know they're good, because there's no mountains at that height. But hovering is different, because we don't have any navigational gauge. We have really nothing telling us where we're at other than the internal navigating system—but that's not going to help you when you're a couple of feet from a sheer rock face." Until the weather cleared, in other words, a hoist was out of the question. *At least we can get the PJs down on the glacier*, Ercolani thought. But they needed to get the helicopter out of there before they became totally socked in.

As soon as the helicopter touched down at base camp, CRO Keen and PJs Strouse and Brister hopped out into the snow and began unloading duffel bags with everything they thought they might need: a litter, climbing gear, static rope for lowering a victim off a ledge. Breun and Peterson took off to wait out the clouds and peeled down toward the valley and the riverbank that John, Alissa, Lauren, and Emmett had hiked up the week before.

Immediately upon jumping out, Brister regretted leaving his snowshoes and warm layers behind. The temperature was around freezing, the air was damp, and the snow remained wet from the day's warmth: textbook hypothermia conditions. They'd start getting cold soon, and they were going to be here for a while.

SOMEHOW, JOHN HAD MANAGED TO LEAD ACROSS THE SLAB TRAverse without slipping off into the mist, and somehow Alissa had managed to cross over, too. Just one more rightward traverse separated them from Lauren. Around then everyone heard the low *whunk whunk whunk* of the helicopter.

The noise of the rotor blades was the sound of salvation. It had taken four and a half hours of effort to get to Lauren. As he climbed, John reached her first. He looked down at the mass of knots his friend had used to tie off the belay.

"When you can't tie knots, tie lots!" he quipped, an attempt to break her reverie to some extent, to bring humanity into an inhumane situation. Alissa followed him up and soon all three were sharing the little sloping ledge that had been Lauren's lonely vigil for five hours. Lauren's state alarmed her friends. Her teeth chattered from the cold. Alissa and John both realized that Lauren, usually competent with technical skills, was very much not herself.

"Do you have any gear?" John asked.

"This is it," Lauren said, pointing to her anchor. "Emmett has everything else."

She'd been hard-pressed to scavenge so much as a carabiner; Emmett had taken it all up with him on lead. John reracked the equipment he had left onto his harness and readied himself to go up to Emmett—but as he did so, a text from Global Rescue pinged in. The helicopter was going to try a maneuver to get their friend out of there.

"We should wait," he said. "They might just be able to get him right now. I don't know if I'm going to be in their way or not."

*Perhaps the rescuers could just snag Emmett and fly away,* John thought. This would save him from having to go up there. To see something he might not want to see. They all stood fast on the little ledge. But the noise from the rotors was growing fainter through the clouds. The rescuers were leaving them. "We could see the lights on the helicopter and we could see that it was roaming around in the base camp. And then all of a sudden it was farther and farther away, and it was a terrible feeling," Lauren remembers. "We just thought they couldn't do it, that they were leaving." She sent a flurry of texts to Global Rescue.

"Very close."

"Further away now."

At 1:18, Global Rescue texted back, citing bad weather and requesting that the climbers get down to base camp on their own.

"They r right below us. We cannot come down," Lauren texted back, frustrated.

Alissa sent a message to Emily, who'd been relaying information to Global Rescue from her apartment in Somerville (the Global Rescue dispatcher would then relay these to the AKRCC). "Please tell the heli that we cannot meet them at basecamp. Emmett must be rescued from the ridge. Please wait out the fog." Nobody allowed themselves to think about what would happen if this couldn't be done, if they were left alone again.

"Our spirits were at their lowest," Alissa says. She and Lauren shouted for the helicopter to come back as the sound of the blades faded. When she'd gotten to the ledge, Alissa tasked herself with taking care of Lauren. One of Alissa's main qualities was her ability to endure hardship without complaint, to project a positive attitude when any situation seemed bleak, to radiate toughness no matter what. Now, she tried to comfort her friend, distracting Lauren from what was occurring above them and out of sight. Lauren had been the most cautious about the trip. It was she who had come up with the rescue plan. And now Lauren was here, waiting on a ledge and living the situation she'd dreaded for months. She looked so different from the happy woman who had posed in base camp hours ago.

Now that the helicopter had flown away, John decided he would try and get up to Emmett after all, and this meant he would have to climb the pitch that had injured his best friend. He didn't dawdle, but the prospect must have terrified him. The accident victims he and Alissa had assisted in the past had been strangers. Caring for a badly injured human calls for a cold sort of calculus: a paradoxical dehumanization of the victim. Could he do that with Emmett? And what if Emmett knocked anything else down? Or what if John pulled on something that would kill Emmett or hurt Lauren and Alissa below? How many more loose blocks were waiting up there? John hadn't allowed himself much time to think about Emmett as he was rappelling. But as he ascended up and to the left, what he was about to do hit him. "I knew I'd have to see him, and he wasn't in a good state. We could tell, just from his body language and the fact that he hadn't been able to move himself. It was a little weird to go up there: That's *Emmett* up there. And I'm not sure what I'm going to see."

John took Alissa's inReach so he could text Lauren and Alissa, who would stay on the ledge below, and prepared to re-lead the section up to where Emmett had fallen. Because Emmett had placed gear every ten feet or so, as John climbed up, he clipped his own red leader rope to the gear his friend had placed before the fall. He remembered thinking that the pitch wasn't very difficult, 5.7 or so, and that Emmett had done a good job protecting it. The rock was crumbly but not overly bad. Emmett's final piece, the one that had arrested his fall, was a number six nut firmly wedged in a crack. John reached Emmett after forty-five minutes of effort. It was now 2:35 in the morning: six and a half hours since Emmett had fallen.

The scene was awful. Emmett had gotten himself into a semi-protected position by instinct, like Norman crawling down on her ledge in Patagonia. He was half lying down, half hanging in the harness. Emmett's helmet had indeed been blown off: either from the fall or from being hit by rock. The little rock shelf he'd gotten himself to was covered in blood. He flailed around but his arms did not seem to be working properly. One arm was broken. The back of Emmett's skull was misshapen—it was clearly broken as well—and he was bleeding from his ear. He was barely responsive. At one point, Emmett clearly said "David"; he thought John was David Roberts. The rest was mostly gibberish. All this confirmed a traumatic brain injury.

John added two cams to the piece that had held Emmett's fall, making an anchor. Next, he pulled up several armloads of rope and clipped this to the anchor, so he had a long tether to move around on without being untied from the mountain. At one point, John tried to feed Emmett, helping put food into his mouth, though Emmett retched this back up instantly. He squeezed Emmett's hand. There was no squeeze back.

"He was going, or was gone," John remembers. If he had felt hope at watching his friend's movements hours earlier, it was now dashed. A helicopter was his only option, but one had just flown away.

*Fuck. He's going to die.*

John sent a desperate text to rescuers: "With Emmett need heli now." There was nothing else he could do. He took out some extra layers from his pack and wrapped them around his friend, tried to make him comfortable, tried to keep him warm.

Then he got as close to Emmett as the sloping ledge would allow and waited.

# FIFTEEN

As John was climbing up to Emmett, a pall settled over Lauren and Alissa. The rescue team had flown away because of the weather and now they were alone again. In what seemed like an unbearable tinge of irony, the fog that had stymied the helicopter had now rolled out and there was an unobstructed view of the base camp again, a thousand feet below.

"And I noticed. Or Alissa did—one of us—in addition to the three colorful tents down there, there were these ants or something," remembers Lauren. "And then we realized they were moving."

"Oh shit! Somebody's down there," Lauren said. Alissa peered down, too. They could see them clearly now. The ants were Keen, Strouse, and Brister. The women began calling to them and the men called back up in response. Earlier, Keenan Zerkel had texted Alissa and asked if they could turn on some kind of light, and the women turned on their phone flashlights, as this was all they had. It was a huge comfort to know they weren't alone.

Below, the three rescuers began following the tracks up toward the climbers. Keen remembers initially thinking that the simplest thing to do would have been to just climb up and grab Emmett and get back down to base camp: Because of the weather, the PJs had not had a good view of the mountain yet and above them was simply unknown terrain. But when the clouds cleared, they could see Lauren and Alissa. They could also see this wasn't easy scrambling terrain, or anything they could waltz up. There was no hope of getting to the injured man quickly.

"We started going up this bowl a mile or so, just postholing up this approach," Brister remembers. "There's rockslide and avalanche debris and we thought: This is a really bad place to be right now." Though they did not know it, some of this debris had likely been knocked off during Emmett's accident hours before.

In the gray, tepid light of early morning, the three rescuers could now see Lauren and Alissa, and the two parties could hear each other, too. "The acoustics were really interesting in this space," Lauren recalls. "Once Adam got dropped off, and he came up and was positioned at the base of the ridge, we could yell to each other." They couldn't believe the men were trying to reach them up the gully.

"Go down! It's too dangerous!" they yelled. On the ledge with Emmett, John heard the muffled shouts, too. There was no way the rescuers could climb up in time. "We need a helicopter *now*," John shouted down from his ledge.

Lauren remembers this yell. "And his voice—he sounded really worried and serious. I don't think I'll ever forget that. We realized Emmett had no time; I think when John went to climb up to him, I wondered whether he was already going to be dead."

BREUN, PETERSON, ERCOLANI, AND GUEDEA WAITED IN THE HELI-copter down in the valley. As the weather moved in and out over the cockpit of the parked Pave Hawk, Breun and the rest of the crew were weighing what they knew of Emmett's injury—chiefly its severity—against the risk they'd incur to try saving him. The waiting was frustrating for everyone but there was nothing they could do about it.

Breun was no stranger to these slow-moving weather systems. He'd grown up in Alaska. Flying had always been a part of his life, but when he was younger, he'd considered being a doctor, like a lot of his mom's family. He'd gone to the White Mountain School in New Hampshire on a skiing scholarship but ended up back in Alaska after that. He'd started working at the Blood Bank of Alaska, even gotten a premed degree in college after joining the navy.

"My dad was a pilot, and I said, Oh, well, maybe I'll check that out," Breun says. "I went down to the National Guard and went off to pilot training and I joined the 210th in November 2000."

The Air National Guard is technically a reserve force, but the word "reserve" meant little in Alaska, where flying two hundred and fifty days a year wasn't unheard of. Like their PJ counterparts, pilots also benefit from this real-world training. Their decisions become second nature. "We have some of the best pilots in the world," Keen tells me. It's a high-pressure job, but Breun's experience and training was equal to the task. "I think that it's just a skill set you learn over time," Breun says. "You mitigate risk. You know what the aircraft is capable of and what the people are capable of. . . . Hey, is this doable, is this in my skill set? Do the people on board have the same skill set? Are you gonna go over the threshold?"

Breun had done missions all over the world. In 2016 he'd been awarded the Jolly Green Giant Association's award for Rescue of the Year for plucking two Saudi pilots out of the Gulf of Aden, lowering a PJ down into pitch-black, yawning seas roiled by a storm. But perhaps the experience that most informed his decision-making in the Hidden Mountains had happened in the first year of his career.

In 2001, Jack Tackle and Charlie Sassara attempted to climb a new route on a remote peak named Mount Augusta, which sits directly on the border between Alaska and the Canadian Yukon. Calling Tackle and Sassara experienced is an understatement; they were grand masters of Alaskan alpinism.

Over a span of thirty years, Tackle had completed more than thirty expeditions to the mountains of Alaska and western Canada. In 1979, his partner, Ken Currens, fell two hundred and fifty feet while attempting a new route on the southeastern side of Denali that they'd dubbed the Isis Face. Currens broke his femur in the fall. Making the difficult decision to leave Currens and get help, Tackle had rappelled alone, returning with a young climber named Mugs Stump, a former college football quarterback who was destined to become one of the most legendary alpinists of his generation. Together, Tackle and Stump climbed back up to the team's previous high point. Currens was alive and they managed to get him down.

Sassara, a native Alaskan, viewed climbing as an extension of his upbringing, of working in the bush or flying with his dad. He climbed the West Rib of Denali in winter, an ascent that ended in tragedy when his partner slid down the rib to his death, nearly knocking Sassara off in the process. In 1997, he and Carlos Buhler finished an eight-thousand-foot knife-edge ridge in the Yukon on a mountain called University Peak. The climb was a perfect execution of alpinism: six days of climbing in sync up a ridge that offered few options for retreat.

Eighteen months before Tackle and Sassara left on their joint 2001 expedition, Tackle had contracted Guillain-Barré syndrome while guiding in South America, which left him nearly paralyzed for fifty-two days. This attempt on Mount Augusta would mark his return to alpinism. Though he and Sassara had never climbed in the big mountains together before, they had known each other for years, part of the tight-knit alpine community that flew to Alaskan peaks each year for first ascents.

The pair picked an ice line that snaked upward for fifteen hundred feet before joining the summit snowfields above. They started at eight in the morning, swapping leads up a gully of ice and snow that split Augusta's north face in two. After climbing difficult ice for twelve hours, Tackle and Sassara managed to get about halfway up the gully. They had reasoned that the cold, north-facing gully would certainly remain frozen, keeping the stones in place. But forest fires had plagued Alaska that year, and a freak temperature inversion rolled in. The mountain began to thaw. They set to work chopping a ledge for their little tent in the ice, trying to cut a spot wide enough for two people before hitting rock underneath. It didn't work. "As often happens when you really need the ice to be thick and fat," Tackle wrote, "we hit rock. The ledge was one person wide."

Tackle took an end of rope and climbed about forty feet in search of a more suitable bivouac spot, finding nothing. The ice was steep and rocky and there wouldn't be anywhere to sleep for the night. As he began to look just one ledge higher, he suddenly blacked out.

"A rock the size of a briefcase had come from the upper part of the face and hit me, literally out of the blue. It hadn't touched the wall for a long time. Charlie saw it silhouetted against the sky as it traveled at terminal velocity into my back. He yelled, but I never heard him."

The force of the blow knocked Tackle into a thirty-foot fall. Sassara lowered him to the ledge.

"The first thing was adrenaline," Sassara says, "just this immense shot of this amazing drug. And you're barely able to control your own body." Sassara hauled his friend into an upright position. "The adrenaline gave me the ability to just take him by the front of the chest; just grab him by the front of his coat and turn him a hundred and eighty degrees and hold him against the wall and tie him in short." Tackle had been hit in the back and head, but he regained consciousness. He was in immense pain. Both men feared Tackle was bleeding internally.

They were twenty-five hundred feet up a mountain. The closest sign of civilization was seventy miles away. Using their collective decades of experience, Tackle and Sassara tried to figure out what to do next, staying calm in order to make rational decisions. Their lives now hinged on the small actions they *could* take, the concrete steps that would inch them toward survival. Sassara discarded any thoughts of desperation. He focused instead on the tasks he could reliably perform in order to improve their situation.

"There was no consideration of anything else. Just do that work." He set up their little tent and put Tackle inside; the small ledge they'd chopped and deemed inadequate moments earlier would have to do. He started melting snow for Tackle to drink. Homing in on these small, immediate, and doable tasks, Sassara worked until there was no more work to be done.

Lowering Tackle remained the simplest option, but Tackle felt as if he was in too much pain to make it down.

So the pair concluded that their best chance lay with Sassara rappelling alone to summon help. A satellite phone stashed in base camp, three thousand vertical feet and two miles away, presented the swiftest line of communication to the outside world. Traversing a glacier alone is a hideously dangerous affair. The yawning crevasses that snake through the Yukon and Alaska are some of the largest in the world. Covered in snow, they are often difficult to detect. If Sassara screwed up a rappel or fell in a hidden crevasse both men would die: Sassara in the maw of the glacier and Tackle stuck on his ledge.

Sassara left whatever he could with Tackle: down jackets, both sleeping bags, the climbing hardware he thought he did not need.

Both men remember the moment the ropes slithered down the snow, separating them, as jarring. Leaving a partner was the most gut-wrenching decision in alpine climbing. "It was difficult for him to know that he was helping me more by leaving than by staying with me on the ledge," Tackle later wrote. "I listened as the ropes pulled softly through the snow. Then, suddenly, it was quiet. The ropes were free of the anchor, and the cord was truly severed."

"It was an incredible sensation," Sassara remembered of leaving the ledge. "The bond was now broken." On the rappels, Sassara focused on what he could do to stay alive, the micro attention to detail he knew would provide the best chance at delivering them both. Another rock careened down and Sassara slipped it the way you'd dodge a punch in a boxing match, waiting and watching to see where it would ricochet down the gully.

Reaching the glacier, he focused on navigating without falling into any crevasses. The sudden warmth was both a blessing and a curse: On the one hand, the melting snow left telltale sags in the glacier where crevasses lurked. But then a fog rolled in and Sassara could no longer make out his camp. Instead, he trained his attention on the profile of Mount Logan in the distance. Below this landmark, he knew, there would be the tents. *Get to this and you're okay,* Sassara remembers thinking.

When he got to the tents, eight hours after leaving the ledge, he made a call on the satellite phone and sent a JPEG of where on the route rescuers could expect to find Tackle. Sassara had left the stove with Tackle, and he realized how thirsty he had become. He began melting water on the spare stove they'd left in base camp, and a mixture of relief and anxiety for his friend flooded him. "I cried. Probably all night," he recalls.

Sassara's wife called Daryl Miller, the south district ranger for Denali National Park. Miller was a legend in Alaska rescue circles, a Vietnam vet with a renowned expedition résumé. Shortly thereafter, a Pave Hawk from the 210th flew over the border into Canada—Miller had obtained permission faster than anyone could have imagined—and, supported by a small group of alpinists and climbing rangers, began searching for Tackle.

On Tuesday—more than a day after Tackle had been hit by the rock—he heard the sound of rotors.

"It was the best helicopter sound I had ever heard. The media images of the Vietnam War during my youth and the sound of helicopters during my years of climbing had always meant something bad. For the very first time, the sound was sublime. In fact, I had never heard anything that made me happier.

"Now I knew two things for sure. They were looking for me, and Charlie was alive in the tent with tons of food and the sat phone, drinking our Scotch. He had made it!" Tackle wrote in an article for *Alpinist*.

Breun sat in the copilot's seat next to Rick Watson, who at thirty-three was one of the youngest pilots in the 176th. The next year, Watson would land a Pave Hawk on Mount Saint Elias at over fourteen thousand feet—an astounding wrangling of an aircraft not designed for flying at altitude. Though a fog bank blanketed Tackle and Sassara's base camp, the weather higher up on the north face remained flyable. At first the rescue team flew past the east face, not the north face where Tackle lay trapped; a bush pilot had made a mistake relaying which side of Augusta Tackle and Sassara had been climbing on. "We were just flying in and out of the clouds all day," Breun recalls. Eventually, though, the C-130, which was also flying around Augusta, spotted the little yellow tent. From the helicopter, the PJ—a surfer turned alpinist named Dave Shuman—and the other rescuers spied Tackle.

"We saw him waving his arms, and it was the first indication that he was still alive in forty-eight hours," Shuman told a podcaster in 2016.

Lowering a rescuer on a wire—what the Alaska Air National Guard calls a high-angle hoist—is a risky game of geometry. A hoist cable is nearly two hundred feet long and the rotor diameter of a Pave Hawk is fifty-two feet. Thus, the steeper the terrain, the closer to a cliff a pilot must inch their helicopter in order to plant a rescuer onto steep terra firma. A rescuer is sent down on a cable to clip in a victim, either to the hoist or to a litter basket.

Helicopter rotors move at a constant speed (258 rpm, in the case of a Pave Hawk). A pilot adjusts the angle of the rotor blades to create more or less lift, thereby gaining or losing altitude. Heavier helicopters need more power to hover. Flight crews need to dump as much extra weight as possible in order to stay put long enough to pick someone off a mountain; this is most easily done by jettisoning fuel and people. Once a rescuer is dangling beneath the helicopter in the complex topography of a mountain environment, maintaining elevation becomes crucial to performing a hoist.

Compared to smaller helicopters, Black Hawks and Pave Hawks are very stable aircraft, but this doesn't mean a low-probability, high-risk scenario can't happen. When a helicopter hovers close enough to a cliff, the draft caused by the rotors can churn up loose debris and send it *through* the rotors—a catastrophic event that would cause the helicopter to drop like a stone. Yet the biggest risk is incurred by the rescuer being lowered underneath the aircraft.

On their first attempt to get Tackle, Tom Dietrich, the flight engineer, began lowering Shuman, but high winds meant the wire began quivering like a bowstring, sending Shuman spinning. In such "extreme emergencies," as the Pave Hawk operations manual calls them, a pilot's best bet is to fly away and place the rescuer on the ground in order to stop their swing. Failing that, a pilot must pick up speed in the helicopter to offset the spinning, "up to 40 knots" with the rescuer still dangling, and this is what Watson did, flying away from Augusta.

"Which at first is a little scary," Shuman admitted in typical PJ understatement, "because one minute you're next to a rock, and the next minute you're looking down twenty-five hundred to three thousand feet, staring down at the glacier."

By the third attempt, Watson was able to steady the helicopter enough by flipping the Pave Hawk around, so that the cockpit was *into* the wind, which was coming from the west. Dietrich would have to lower Shuman from the opposite side of the flight deck. He'd have nothing, except the considerable expanse of the Yukon, to use as a reference.

But it worked. Shuman pendulumed in about twenty feet below Tackle's bivouac tent.

"As soon as Dave hit the snow, he sprinted up to me while still attached to the wire and ripped open the door of the tent," Tackle recalled in his *Alpinist* article. "'We've got thirty seconds to do this!' he screamed."

Tackle and Shuman raced to untie from the mountain. They slid like penguins down the slope, with Tackle in searing pain. Watson eased the helicopter down to help absorb the shock of the two men suddenly loading the cable. (Unlike a climbing rope, which is rated for a dynamic load, a hoist cable can only handle six hundred pounds.) If the weight was too great, the line, made of woven steel, would snap.

They flew off as quickly as they could. "Tom Dietrich later told me that the idiot lights were flashing on the dashboard when the helicopter docked. The chopper was out of gas," Tackle wrote. "The alpine bond: Trust. Every one of those guys was risking their lives to save mine. A combination of gratitude and humility filled my heart."

"We had to get gas right away and we went down the mountain with them still on the hoist, reeling them up as we went," Breun recalls. "That one was a little sporty." Shuman and Tackle made it into the cabin as the Pave Hawk flew toward the Hercules C-130 to refuel.

Shuman acknowledged in his 2016 interview that these types of incidents only come along once in a blue moon. Vertical terrain and technical rescues are the exception, not the norm. And beyond all of the knowledge and experience and external considerations, hoists take a little luck. It's not unlike climbing in that you can do everything right and still end up with a catastrophe.

This might all sound wild to a layperson, and it is. Yet to pilots who train and know their machines and what they can do, or to alpinists with as much experience as Tackle and Sassara, these real risks are weighed against decades of experience and thousands of hours of flying or climbing.

"If you're not still scared sometimes, then you're doing it wrong, you know?" Breun notes. It's likely the pilots, PJs, and everyone else at Elmendorf compartmentalize risk and fear the same way good climbers do. They *use* it, and it informs their decision-making. "It's not a lack of fear that separates elite performers from the rest of us. They're afraid, too, but they're not overwhelmed by it. They manage fear," Laurence Gonzales writes in *Deep Survival*. Sassara and Tackle ignored the big things they couldn't control and focused on what they could: melt water, set up the tent. A few days later, their rescuers did the same exact thing.

According to Breun: "You have a wife and kids and a dog and a mortgage payment or whatever, but boy, now there's a rescue: You just click everything else off and you're just focused on that one thing you're supposed to do. And when you're the aircraft commander, you're in charge of everybody. You have the extra weight on you to make and have sound judgment."

SEVENTEEN YEARS LATER, TACKLE'S RESCUE WAS AMONG COUNT-less others that informed Breun and the flight crew's decision-making. Down in the valley below Mount Sauron, getting the weather to cooperate in order to grab Emmett seemed like a pipe dream. But just in case, Ercolani scribbled calculations in the back of the Pave Hawk, writing in the glow of the cabin with a pencil, trying to figure out how much torque and power the helicopter would need to maintain the altitude to get Emmett off the wall.

Finally, at around three in the morning, about two hours after the rescuers had first landed on the snowfield, Keen radioed from base camp. The weather seemed good enough to try for another hoist. The Pave Hawk jettisoned most of its fuel and zipped up into the cirque. From the cabin, Ercolani could see the mountain for the first time. It looked steep.

*How are we gonna do this?* he wondered.

But by the time the Pave Hawk flew past the base camp, the weather had socked in again. The helicopter hovered for as long as it could, then flew off to refuel from the C-130. This repeated again: The crew flew up, the weather closed in, and the Pave Hawk had to hook up to the Herc and fly back down to the valley.

Lauren, John, and Alissa could do nothing but sit and wait. The four climbers had been on the mountain for twenty-two hours. "It was stressful when the helicopter was making these attempts and not successful," Lauren says. Everyone knew there could only be so many attempts. In base camp, Keen considered another option, though he didn't want to. If the weather never cleared, they'd try to climb up and get Emmett that way. It would also take upward of twelve hours, and Emmett would probably be dead by the time they managed to lower him.

Brister and Strouse remained uphill, higher on the snowfield, between Keen and the climbers. Brister was beginning to get cold. The men had struggled uphill earlier, dragging a two-part titanium litter through the snow to the base of the mountain. Now they had not moved in more than an hour, and Brister was wearing little more than a lightweight Patagonia windbreaker. Their sweat was freezing. He regretted not having anything warm to put on. Worse, though, was the thought of having to climb up and get Emmett in the fog without the helicopter.

Reaching that point on the mountain had taken the climbers twelve hours the day before—in the sun, with proper gear, rested. The PJs would be carrying extra ropes and the pounds of other gear needed to lower an injured man down the mountain. And once they reached Emmett, they'd have to set up anchors and lower him down the loose, angulated terrain the climbers had dreaded descending.

As a general rule, the steeper the terrain, the easier it is to lower someone in a litter. The closer this angle gets to zero degrees, the more drag a rope system creates. Being a litter attendant is taxing in the best scenarios. The thing bashes against shins and kneecaps. The team above, hauling or lowering, can kick loose stones down.

In steep, vertical terrain, rescuers can use the wall to guide themselves, and the static lines have much less chance of dislodging anything. But inching a litter through the angled, jumbled blocks of Sauron would be a nightmare, with plenty of chances for a rope to snag on a loose block or for more rocks to become dislodged along the way. The last thing anyone wanted was another injured person. If the helicopter couldn't attempt a hoist, though, the PJs would at least try this option.

John had been on the ledge with Emmett for three hours now. He didn't say much, and what he'd texted to his friends had been vague and tinged with urgency. Lauren and Alissa did not know if Emmett was still alive. Alissa tried to keep Lauren talking and warm. It was all she could do: keep her friend's mind off the fact that Emmett was dying a pitch above her. Alissa asked routine questions. *How was her brother doing?* Lauren would reply in a monotone.

At around four thirty in the morning, Keen radioed the C-130 and told the two PJs on board to get ready to parachute into the cirque with more climbing gear. They'd need to try to climb up to Emmett. Keen had just prepared a drop zone when the Pave Hawk crew radioed down.

The sky was clear. It was now or never. "The other two PJs were literally on the ramp getting ready to exit," Brister says. "They were about to get the biggest mission of their lives—jump into a mountain pass—when the aircraft commander says hold on, we're gonna make one more attempt with the hoist."

Brister and Strouse slid down the approach on their butts, wet, tired, yet filled again with adrenaline, and the Pave Hawk once again landed at the base of Sauron. "You want this one?" Strouse asked. Brister's eyes nearly jumped out of their sockets. But he wanted it.

In order to shave weight, Strouse and Keen stayed in the climbers' base camp. Once on board, Brister clipped into the hoist apparatus. In an ideal world, he would have gone down on the hoist with the litter and stabilized Emmett—or at the very least gotten a cervical collar on Emmett's neck for the hoist—but this was a far cry from an ideal world.

Breun brought the Pave Hawk up in a slow hover, as close as he dared to the mountain. The fog that had stymied them still threatened to close in on the peak. "We evaluated power and timeline, and we knew Emmett had been there for six, maybe even eight hours at that point. And we knew he couldn't do that for too much longer. We decided to take a chance on the weather, and I think God helped us out a little bit. . . . So we started hovering up, and hovering up. And we got to the point where it was . . . I would say dangerously close to the mountain."

From the cockpit, everyone could make out the figures more clearly. Lauren and Alissa were waving at the flight crew as they flew higher to John and Emmett and hovered close to Sauron.

The Pave Hawk flies into the little cirque.
*(Credit: Alissa Doherty)*

"We were pretty damn close," Ercolani remembers. The clock began ticking. "We've got to do this now," he told Brister. He started lowering the PJ down. Now everyone onboard was fully committed to the hoist.

"With the vibration and the noise and the harmonics you're always worried about something coming through the rotor system, which would have been pretty catastrophic," Breun explains.

Breun kept the helicopter as steady as he could. "White knuckling it, you know, just squeezing the crap out of the controls and you're thinking, *Please God, don't let a rock come through here, don't let snow come through, don't let anything happen.*"

Below the machine, Brister dangled like a spider, hovering above the climbers. The two little figures on the peak got closer and closer. John, exhausted, eyes hollowed out. Emmett wrapped in John's extra jackets to stay warm.

To John, Brister appeared as this otherworldly figure dangling in the sky. But then he noticed—of all absurd things—that Brister was wearing the same footwear he was, bright orange climbing boots made by the Italian company Scarpa. *This guy's a climber*, he remembers thinking. *He's just a guy.* Somehow, the boots humanized Brister for John. As the PJ got closer, John clasped a firm hand onto Brister's rescue vest and swung him onto the little ledge, now ricocheting with small stones and dust and debris from the rotor wash.

Up in the cockpit, Breun had such little visibility that he was reduced to a spot on the cliff, mere feet from the rotor. He focused on that one spot, and some little purple wildflowers became his only frame of reference. He asked his copilot, Seth Peterson, if he could take over flying for a second, but he couldn't—sitting in the left-hand side of the helicopter, he had no visual gauge to steady the Pave Hawk with. "While we were there the weather came in and out," Breun remembers. "At one point Seth said, well, we can't go anywhere right now, because there's nothing to look at: essentially instrument conditions."

As the clouds floated past the helicopter, Brister got situated, using one hand to keep himself close to the mountain while working with the other. He'd wanted to secure Emmett with more than his harness, but this wasn't an option given their limited timeframe, and he clipped Emmett's harness into the hoist above him instead. Next, Brister took his knife out and cut Emmett's blue climbing rope below the knot he'd been tied in with all day. "At this point," he explains, "I should have taken a pause," meaning he should have taken a deliberate instant to stop and take stock. There's a saying rescuers use: "Slow is smooth and smooth is fast." When you're in it, it's hard to see what's going on. That's why mountain rescuers designate a safety officer to walk through and check each component of a rope system, or why avalanche searchers assign a person to stand back and observe the bigger picture instead of searching with a beacon. But all this was happening in a flash, and Brister was operating by himself without the luxuries of extra time. He was given seconds to make life-and-death decisions.

Ercolani watched from the cabin, controlling the hoist, and Brister swung out, cradling Emmett as best he could. But from Ercolani's confusing vantage point, looking straight down with little depth perception, the PJ's back was in the way, and he had no idea whether or not Emmett was clipped to anything.

"I was hoping to ease him on out," Brister recalls. But as Brister and Emmett swung out, John was being pulled from the mountain, too. Something was wrong.

When John had clipped in and built an anchor, he'd used part of his rope as a tether and pulled up the rest while he tended to Emmett. Now, in the confusion, Brister, Emmett, and John were all ensnared in this mess of spare rope. Brister and Emmett weren't actually tied into John's line at all, it was just wrapped around them—as if they'd run through a clothesline—but all three were connected to one another, the mountain, and the helicopter. John was being lifted into the air by the helicopter hoist, too.

From the cabin, Ercolani stared at the mess of rope with dread. If the men couldn't get free themselves, Ercolani would have to release the cable from the hovering helicopter—what's known as "shearing" the hoist. Ercolani was counting the seconds, hoping Brister could solve the problem before it came to that.

"Hey dude, we've gotta go now," Breun radioed Ercolani from the cockpit.

"In aviation you always want to have a backup plan. But sometimes you're definitely committed. And we had options, but the options were pretty grim," Ercolani says.

Down below, Brister had a radio but not a free hand to use it. He tried to go for his knife while John also fumbled for his, a teeny little blade for cutting cord. They'd have to cut John's rope and hope it'd all work out. The seconds felt like hours, but Ercolani didn't shear the cable, and Breun sat tight. Everyone trusted one another.

Brister managed to grab a Benchmade rescue hook from his chest rig first, and with that, sliced one end of John's rope, hoping he hadn't cut John's tether. A split second of eye contact, then John nodding and that was that.

"I cut the rope and we swung out again. Thank God we were able to get off and away from the mountain. Luckily John was fine," Brister says. "I'm glad I was with a veteran crew and a really skilled flight engineer; they had the patience and the wherewithal to say, Hold on, he's hung up."

John, still tied to the mountain, was now alone on the ledge. Emmett and Brister were free. Ercolani, maintaining just the right amount of tension on the cable, reeled them up as Breun flew back away from the peak.

As he was being winched toward the cabin, Brister tried to keep

Emmett's head and neck protected in midair as Ercolani tried to keep them from spinning on the cable. By the time Brister reached the cabin, he was shaking from the effort and adrenaline. "That hoist felt like it took twenty minutes, but it was probably twenty seconds."

The last time Lauren had seen Emmett had been more than nine hours ago, after they'd snapped a photo and he climbed around the corner of the ridge and out of her view. As the rescue happened above them, Lauren and Alissa could see the Pave Hawk hovering but they couldn't see Brister, Emmett, or John, so they remained unaware of how things were playing out. The rotor wash sent pebbles and dirt flying down toward them, but Alissa was mostly worried about Lauren. The longer he'd stayed up there, the more urgent John's yells had become. Alissa, reading the cues in her partner's voice, had wondered to herself if Emmett was already dead, if John had not wanted to say that in Lauren's earshot.

"When Adam took off with Emmett . . . I didn't want her to see his dead body. I tried to keep her head down. And she looked up anyway."

"They swung into view for a moment, and that was the first time I had seen Emmett since the fall. And that was really intense," Lauren remembers. "They hadn't been able to stabilize him because there was nowhere to work . . . and he was just like a rag doll."

# PART III

# SIXTEEN

In the spring of 2018, eager to return to climbing after having shoulder surgery turned me into a runner for a year, I booked two trips for myself. The first began in April, a few months before Emmett, Lauren, John, and Alissa embarked on their own expedition. I'd flown to the Great Gorge of Ruth Glacier, in the central Alaska Range. Having hardly climbed since surgery, I wasn't certain how well my shoulder would manage in the mountains, especially with a pack on. I figured I'd always be able to bow out and read in base camp if it got bad. In total, we were a group of eight, an eclectic mix of friends and acquaintances. Some had climbed in Alaska before, others had not. A pilot who worked for Talkeetna Air Taxi dropped us off on the glacier.

On my first trip to the Great Gorge I'd been a twenty-two-year-old with lofty ambitions and zero understanding of death or of what it would mean for my loved ones if it came for me. Now, I proceeded with a caution I'd not had before. However, my return trip in 2018 quickly became one of my favorites. Though horrible snow conditions thwarted us—and everyone else—in the Great Gorge that season, we came within striking distance of some dreamy summits. The jagged peaks seemed scary in a way they had not been before, when my inexperience meant I deciphered little of the mountains' actual hazards, and when I'd climbed without the fear that now tugged me toward base camp.

Failure is relative in the mountains and we still climbed thousands of feet of terrain. Some of the climbing was downright terrifying, our crampons and ice axes skidding down through unconsolidated sugar snow before sparking the granite underneath. On a peak called Mount Bradley, my buddy Elliot was nearly killed by a slab avalanche as it fractured all around him. We shook it off, but after trying to force it through a few more pitches without gear and in similar snow, we retreated. Though some of the climbing was puckering and dangerous, some of it was magnificent. On our last attempt, trying to repeat a route that had seen just a few ascents, we gained a ridge awash in sun. The long, evening light sifted through the Alaska Range, the tips of the peaks reflecting their shadows like sundials on the glaciers below. The views were as good as the climbing. We moved bare-handed along perfect alpine granite, thousands of feet of snow and ice and quiet looming beneath us. We whooped and hollered with joy. I was back; this felt like home.

*I love this*, I thought to myself. After nearly a month, the two remaining stragglers and I boarded a De Havilland Beaver and flew home. Our lack of success didn't disappoint us (it is Alaska, after all). But the simplicity of being so enmeshed in our surroundings, the ease of only worrying about eating and drinking and not falling, was addicting and enchanting.

I realized I no longer dreamed of climbing the line everyone ogled in photographs. Trips like that one to Ruth Glacier, ones that toed the line but were ultimately moderate adventures, felt like more than enough. Though the mountains would always roar through my heart, I didn't want to chase the big, scary objectives like I once did, and I hoped that climbing would settle in its place next to marriage, next to work, next to life. I didn't want to die, but I couldn't live without the mountains. Climbing was so good when it all went well.

From a risk management standpoint, my second trip of 2018 was a lot less stressful, and it also had the benefit of being just as much fun. In June, I headed to Skaha Bluffs Provincial Park in British Columbia, to rock climb with my father, who had taught me to climb years ago. An assortment of old friends and acquaintances rounded out our motley team, David and Sharon Roberts among them. Ed Ward, who'd been one of David's partners as a young man and had been a constant backpacking and climbing mentor when I was a kid, came too, still all sinew and free of body fat, even in his mid-seventies. David, reeling from the effects of chemotherapy, gamely tied in to the rope as often as he was able. Matt Hale, a constant friend of David's after their Huntington tragedy, still tiptoed up 5.10 slab. Some of these guys had climbed together for more than fifty years. I hoped my partners and I would all live—and tolerate one another—long enough to do the same.

The week was wonderful. My forearms felt more tired from twisting open wine bottles than pulling on rock, but I did manage to coax a few folks out of bed early to chase more difficult climbs.

One night, relaxing on a vineyard—not normally a staple of my spartan expeditions—David grilled me about risk and climbing.

"Do you think it's worth it? Mountain climbing?" he asked. His eyes, hollowed out by cancer, bored into mine from behind his oversized glasses.

"No," I answered flatly. He paused for a second. Ed Bernd's death had not been the only one in his career.

"That was the conclusion I came to." He stopped. "But then I kept doing it."

I laughed. I knew that feeling. It was one thing to talk about quitting. Climbers often vowed to put it all behind them, the way trail runners vowed to quit running while on the last leg of an ultramarathon. It was another thing to actually quit. I told him I no longer desired difficult routes in big mountains. I didn't want to be killed and so that meant dialing it back. I'd still go on climbing trips, but my drive had tempered; the peaks I wanted to climb were smaller, less ambitious ones. As I said this out loud, I wasn't sure if it was really true or just a nice sentiment.

"One thing I've noticed is that there's this terrible randomness," I said, emboldened by the wine and the growing darkness. "It just doesn't matter. You could get killed rappelling two minutes from your house, or you could get killed on some new route. Good climbers die, bad ones die. It's pointless to try and parse any of it. It's all sad, it's all random."

David and Sharon continued climbing through the rest of the trip, making their way up 5.6s and 5.7s despite the searing heat and David's cancer. He must have felt mortality lapping at his heels, burning him to climb just one more chunk of rock. He was very sick then. Sometimes he'd retreat to his room in the condominium and not come out for hours; the worry on Sharon's face when she'd emerge was a marker of her husband's health.

More than anything else, occasional news from his four young friends, who were in the Hidden Mountains as we were in Skaha, bolstered David's mood. Before beginning their attempt on Sauron, on June 22nd, John had sent his text to the Robertses: "Hello from base camp, friends! Forgive us this contact to the outside world but weather is looking magnificent tomorrow and we're excited for what lays ahead. Hope you're enjoying Skaha! We have many stories to share when we reconvene ☺." David had beamed with a fatherly pride when he'd gotten the text.

"They never imagined they'd go on a trip like that," he said. "And here they are, about to climb a new route." Lauren, Emmett, John, and Alissa's presence in the Hidden Mountains was perhaps, to David, a reassurance that, despite his own mortality, adventures could still be mined on this earth if you tried hard enough. David showed us photos the four climbers had sent him. They were crowded into a booth at an Anchorage pub called the Bear Tooth, taken the day before they had flown to the Hidden Mountains. Lauren leans in to nuzzle Emmett's shoulder and he holds a beer up to the camera in a big, grinning "cheers."

I'd never met John and Alissa. But I had met Lauren and Emmett a few times: once at a slideshow I'd given in Cambridge and once again ice climbing on my home crag, Cathedral Ledge, with my buddy Clint Helander, one of the better Alaskan alpinists of his generation. We were planning a trip together and wanted to make sure we climbed well with each other (Clint's nice way of seeing if I could keep up with him or not). A smart-looking couple walked up to us.

"Are you Michael and Clint?" I, at least, was not used to being recognized. I stared at the handsome pair, trying to place them.

"We're Lauren and Emmett!" Recognition dawned—David had talked about them a lot—and we chatted for a little while, swinging our arms and legs in the cold. We pointed them toward a cool climb a little off the beaten path before we started up our own. They seemed happy, in love, fit. I was struck by how honest both seemed to be about their perceived ability level. They didn't want to push it or take risks; they just wanted to have fun, bubbling with a kind of self-deprecating energy that made you want to grab a beer or sit around a campfire with them. Both seemed over the moon to be out climbing, no matter what the climb was.

ON JUNE 24TH, I FLEW HOME FROM SKAHA ALONE WHILE MY DAD met my mom for a road trip up the BC coastline. In my haste and inattention, I'd booked a twelve-hour layover. In Toronto I curled up on a few benches, tossed a jacket over myself, and tried to sleep. Waking up, I saw the figures of David, Sharon, and Ed shuffling through the airport; despite leaving Vancouver a day later, they'd caught up to me. I yelled and chased them down, a little sheepish at having sat in the airport for so long. It was good to see them again.

The early-morning sun dappled through the panes of the airport windows. Bleary, blinking, I bought a few coffees. David passed around that morning's *New York Times*.

"You might be the only person left in the world who reads a physical copy of the paper," I teased before snatching the front page, grateful for the company.

Our plane landed in Boston at 9:35 a.m., the thrum of traffic and the thick New England air hitting us like a wall as we schlepped our bags out of the terminal. David and Sharon shared a taxi with me and dropped me at the bus station. I hugged them both, wondering if I'd ever see David again. They looked exhausted, totally done in from the trip and travel. Once back in New Hampshire, I collapsed on the couch, sinking into the humidity. I cracked open a beer and tried to read, struggling to keep my eyes open. Suddenly the phone rang. It was David. I must have forgotten something in the taxi. Or maybe he was just checking to make sure I hadn't fallen asleep and veered off of Route 16 on the drive north.

"Emmett's fallen." His voice rasped on the other end of the line. "This is all my fault." He kept repeating that. "They never would have gone if I hadn't made them."

"Wait, what? Slow down."

"He took a hundred-foot fall. They rescued him. He's in the hospital right now. It sounds really bad."

*Fuck*, I thought. David had shouldered enough guilt for one lifetime. With all he dealt with, blaming himself for this accident seemed like one final, cruel turn, like his mind had reverted to 1965, alone on the ledge after Ed Bernd's fall.

"Can you call anyone in Anchorage that might know more?"

A few of my climbing partners lived in Anchorage. I called all three of them. Clint sent everyone an article the *Anchorage Daily News* had posted the day before. Based on the timeline and length of fall reported, I felt certain Emmett would die—even if he was now in the hospital.

# SEVENTEEN

Around 5:15 a.m. Alaska time on June 24th, the same morning I began my travels home from Skaha, Corey Ercolani reeled Adam Brister and Emmett up the hoist. Brister cradled Emmett on his lap in midair, holding him as best he could. "I remember actually smelling fuel before we even got the doors closed," Brister says, a sign of how little the helicopter still had on board. Breun landed in base camp, where Keen and Strouse quickly loaded in gear and climbed inside.

The pilots found a sucker hole through the clouds and Ercolani radioed the HC-130 Hercules. One last time, the Pave Hawk hooked up to the plane and took on enough fuel to fly home. Anchorage Air Route Traffic Control Center approved an immediate landing at Providence Alaska Medical Center.

By the time Brister was back in the cabin of the Pave Hawk, his hands were covered in blood from holding the back of Emmett's head. Like John, he noticed Emmett's hands were in a decorticate state—curled awkwardly around themselves—a sign of severe brain damage.

While the Pave Hawk escaped the bad weather of the Hidden Mountains, the rescuers toiled in the crowded rear cabin to keep Emmett alive. Working room was hard to come by. The PJs fastened him into a Stokes litter. He was hypothermic and cold to the touch. A huge contusion on the back of his head where his skull had fractured was hidden beneath a mass of tangled hair. His arm was broken. But most grievous of all was Emmett's neck, which felt deformed and appeared to be broken.

Keen, Ercolani, and Guedea passed the two PJs anything they needed. Strouse held Emmett's head and spine and worked a cervical collar onto his neck. Brister went to work with a pair of trauma shears, cutting away climbing gear and clothing. He also got an IV going—no easy task in the back of a moving helicopter.

To add to the confusion, as he cut away Emmett's harness, Brister knocked over Emmett's open chalk bag. "His chalk bag just exploded," Brister recollects. "It was like *Scarface* in the back of the helo." If the situation hadn't been so serious, it might have been downright funny.

"It was a little chaotic in there," Keen acknowledges. Aside from chalk, the air was thick with adrenaline. The men had just undertaken one of the spookiest hoists of their careers, but no one had time to dwell on any of this. They had a critical patient and forty-five minutes of flight time back to Anchorage.

"I'll be honest," Ercolani remembers of the flight back, "I kind of had . . ." he stops himself. "I don't want to say *panic*. But I was having a good adrenaline overdose. My heart was beating very fast." The flight crew worried about Emmett, but they also worried about the three climbers they'd left on the mountain. Under ideal circumstances, they'd have rescued all four. Global Rescue texted Lauren to relay the message: They'd have to get down by themselves.

When the Pave Hawk landed at Providence Alaska Medical Center in Anchorage at around 6:15 a.m., doctors and nurses scrambled to receive their new patient. With more than four hundred beds and a staff of a thousand, Providence is by far the biggest medical center in Alaska and one of the state's largest employers. And because of the nature of injuries that tend to take place in Alaska, Providence houses one of the finest trauma care centers in the world, ready to receive all manner of grisly wilderness injuries.

The PJs and hospital staff wheeled Emmett in on a stretcher from the helipad, racing him to an elevator and then down to the operating room, where they passed him off to a team led by Benjamin Rosenbaum, a neurosurgeon who rotated among several Anchorage facilities.

In order to reduce the swelling in Emmett's brain, Rosenbaum performed a decompressive craniotomy, removing a chunk of Emmett's skull to create space to relieve the pressure. The intracranial pressure that comes from the swelling of the brain kills the majority of TBI patients. Rosenbaum had no idea if he'd operated on Emmett too late. Even if the surgery was successful there was no telling if Emmett would have much left in the way of cognitive function.

The Pave Hawk flew to Elmendorf. "I always get these really bad headaches after the adrenaline wears off," Brister observes. Back at the section, there were high fives and handshakes, then the team stumbled into town to find breakfast.

When Brister had rushed Emmett's litter through the hospital, down an elevator, and into the operating room, he'd wondered why everyone had been staring at him. On his return to the helicopter, he stopped and looked down. He was coated in Emmett's chalk and blood. And the crampons he'd worn all day were still attached to his feet. He'd been so gripped he'd forgotten to take them off.

WHEN THE NATIONAL GUARD HELICOPTER FLEW EAST, THE LITTLE cirque became silent again. The predawn gloom retreated and sunlight flooded the peaks, just as the forecast had said it would. Lauren, John, and Alissa stared down at their base camp, a thousand feet below. At first, all three were awash in relief. "I was so happy Emmett was in their hands at this point," John remembers. But he also worried the rescue had happened too late. He reasoned his friend had a fifty-fifty chance of making it. "He was less and less responsive as the hours went by that we were together. So I could tell things weren't great. Like, it was cold up there. When they plucked him off, he was deteriorating and he probably couldn't have made it a whole lot longer."

John gathered the gear he'd grabbed from Emmett and that he had used to secure the pitch. In spite of Brister's quick work with his rescue knife, John had the better part of his rope as well as Emmett's. He tied the two ends together and rappelled down to Lauren and Alissa. When he arrived at the small belay stance, John didn't say much, but lingering in the quiet was the question neither Alissa nor Lauren wanted to ask: *Was the helicopter too late?* Alissa wondered to herself if John's silence was confirmation that Emmett had died. What would this news do to Lauren? They all still needed to get down to base camp. They arranged the rope that hadn't been cut in the hoist and threaded it through Lauren's anchor, their first step in working down to the tents.

Ercolani wasn't the only one worried about John, Alissa, and Lauren descending. While the helicopter hovered, Lauren and Alissa had discussed the hopeful possibility of Lauren also getting on so she could be with Emmett as he was flown to the hospital. This would ease John and Alissa's descent, too. "I was wondering: Is she hypothermic? Can she make it down by herself?" Alissa remembers.

John led the rappels without saying much, absorbed in the

technical chore before him and relieved to have this concrete task to occupy his mind, like Charlie Sassara had been on Mount Augusta. On the second-to-last rappel, John hammered in a big piton and tied it off with a small cam. He rappelled first and hunted around for another place to build an anchor.

When Lauren set up her rappel device and leaned back, this piton popped out. The shock load on the system sent her tumbling for a second into the snow, though the second piece of gear, the cam, held. She stood up again. The terrain was low-angle enough that it wasn't catastrophic, certainly not compared to what they'd just been through. Lauren remembers almost laughing the incident off: No one had the bandwidth left to stress about a piton pulling out of the rock anymore. Alissa put a new piece in to back up the anchor and they kept going. But the slip was an acute reminder. They were grappling for control.

At 6:57 a.m., Keenan Zerkel texted Alissa again, asking for contact information for Emmett's family. Emmett was in the operating room. Zerkel's text was the first confirmation John, Alissa, and Lauren had that he was still alive.

# EIGHTEEN

A t some point soon, Tom Miller and Emily Matys knew they'd need to contact Emmett's family. Together, the couple had weathered the night and into the early-morning hours in their Watertown apartment. Their vigil was an odd side effect of modern rescue. Here they were, forty-five hundred miles away, receiving texts from their friends as they battled through the worst night of their lives.

Lauren had texted Emily just after she'd contacted Global Rescue. At the time, the Western States Endurance Run, a hundred-mile trail race, was underway in California. The event had begun just before the four climbers woke up and began their ascent in the Hidden Mountains, and Emily was cheering on a runner, in live time, who'd never completed the challenge before. She had dozed off on the couch that night, and the text from Lauren's inReach woke her. She then woke Tom up, and they started calling phone numbers: the National Park Service, Global Rescue.

Emily felt a connection despite the distance. "I just remember putting myself in that situation, and I just kept saying 'We're here with you,' or something like that. That's how I was feeling, anyway.

I think I was the one that was texting, more so than Tom. "I can just imagine, if Tom had fallen, how I would feel."

"The more we learned, the less optimistic we were," Tom says.

The questions about Emmett's condition still outweighed the few answers they'd received. What little information had trickled in early that morning wasn't promising. Hoping for more details, they waited to call Jessi, Dora, and Emmett III.

"We wanted them to be able to get out to Alaska as soon as possible, but we also didn't want to call them while Emmett was stuck on a mountain and while we didn't know what was wrong," Emily remembers. So they decided to wait until Emmett had been dropped off at Providence. First, Tom called Jessi, who was in her house across the street from her parents, taking it easy after going out for a friend's birthday the night before. Jessi didn't recognize the New Hampshire area code and she ignored Tom's calls several times before answering.

"There's been an accident. Emmett fell. We don't really know anything," Tom told her.

Jessi walked into her kitchen and collapsed on the floor.

"Do you want to tell your parents?" Tom asked. Jessi felt she wouldn't be able to do so. So Tom hung up, steeled himself once again, and called Dora Lyman. She picked up. Fog still clung to the warm summer air. Emmett III was mowing the lawn on the other side of their four-acre property. He remembers Dora walking out to him across the grass.

"Something's happened to Emmett," she said, though it wasn't quite clear what this meant. Dora had been calm on the phone, Emily remembers. "She was obviously concerned and devastated, but she handled it really well. . . . Other people could receive a call like that and just completely break down." Jessi soon came over and the three of them struggled to process the news.

Dora called the hospital, and in the early afternoon she and

Emmett reached Dr. Rosenbaum. Emmett began scribbling notes of what was known about the accident: "30-foot fall on rock. An MRI has been done."

"You should fly up here, and you should be prepared to say goodbye," Dora and Emmett recall Dr. Rosenbaum telling them.

Because the Lymans had planned on spending time in Juneau the following week for the family reunion, they were able to wrangle a last-minute ticket change from the airline for later that day. Jessi got a ticket for the next day. By 4:30 p.m., Dora and Emmett boarded a flight from Bradley International Airport to Anchorage.

A LITTLE BEFORE TEN IN THE MORNING, LAUREN, JOHN, AND ALISSA reached base camp. They'd been climbing for twenty-six hours and awake for far longer. They trudged back to the tents, their heads thundering with a dull, numb exhaustion. Their camp looked like it had been ransacked. The helicopter's rotor wash had flattened the tents and wrenched the guylines loose.

Alissa texted Emily: "We don't have any updates on Emmett. I'm not sure if we should? We have a four day hike out and we're trying to keep Lauren's spirits up. She hasn't asked." After setting the tents back and cooking a much-needed meal, everyone tried to sink into some hollow semblance of sleep.

At five thirty in the evening Emily texted Alissa. Emmett was still alive and he was out of the operating room after having brain surgery. He was conscious but heavily sedated. Once he was more stable they'd perform an operation on his spine. John, Alissa, and Lauren planned on simply hiking out the way they'd come in. That is, until Tony Bannock, Zerkel's friend and the Regal Air employee, reached out to them again. He could get a helicopter in there to pick them up the next day.

That evening, John and Lauren hiked back down to their cache at the base of the snowfield. They grabbed Emmett's shotgun and a few other items they'd not bothered to lug all the way up the hill with them the week before. The next morning, a private charter helicopter picked them up. Alissa and John remember the pilot feeling so bad for their plight that he went the extra mile to make sure they had a memorable return flight, zipping through mountains and hovering near some moose. It felt surreal after what had happened the day before.

At some point on the ride back, Lauren checked her phone, which now had service. Already, press reports were swirling about the accident. Lauren read them with a mixture of anger and dread. "In this fucked-up way I don't really understand," Lauren says, "they had Emmett's name in them."

"Climber badly hurt in fall in remote Southwest Alaska mountains," the *Anchorage Daily News* headline read. A few of the article's details were wrong. The paper reported, for instance, that Emmett had fallen a hundred feet, not thirty. "The climber, identified by troopers as Emmett Lyman, 40, suffered 'severe trauma' and was taken to Providence Alaska Medical Center hospital in critical condition," the article continued.

A Canadian climbing magazine reworded the article before posting it on their website. To Lauren, who had always been a private person, losing control of the accident's narrative so quickly felt like a mental broadside. This was not the return to civilization everyone was expecting.

By the time the trio had landed back in Anchorage, Emmett's parents had arrived, and a friend of their uncle's offered them a spare house to stay in for as long as was needed. Lauren's parents flew up, too. No one knew how long any of this would last and Emmett's survival remained tenuous. If he regained any cognitive function after the craniotomy, it would be a minor miracle.

Over the following days, Emmett would sometimes come to,

but mostly he was unconscious and comatose. On June 27th, Emmett underwent a second surgery, this time for his snapped vertebrae, which were fused back together. It was clear to the medical team that Emmett had received massive trauma to his neck and would likely never walk again.

All Dora cared about was being there for her son. "He was in a coma, and we were just sitting there waiting for him to wake up. Knowing that there was somebody there that knew him was important to me." The days began to trickle together: an incessant cacophony of beeping machines under the fluorescent glow of hospital lights.

Details surrounding Emmett's fall and the daring rescue that followed rippled throughout the local adventure community. Over the following weeks, a band of Anchorage citizens worked to get Emmett's family whatever help they could muster. Two of these were a pair of friends and climbing partners: David Stevenson and Charlie Sassara—the same man who had skied to the satellite phone from Mount Augusta's north face in 2001 in order to rescue Jack Tackle. Sassara had met a few of the PJs involved in saving Emmett and he offered to do whatever he could to help. Stevenson, an author and a professor of creative writing at the University of Alaska Anchorage, worked not far from Providence. Both he and Sassara comprehended the subtleties of what Lauren, John, Alissa, and their families might be going through in ways that others may not have. The men offered their houses, meals, their dogs for comfort: any shard of familiarity or routine or connection that might ease the long days and nights of waiting. Because of their experience in the mountains, both men provided a mental safe haven that was especially meaningful to Lauren.

"Welcome to the club," Sassara told her when they first met. "It's not a club you want to be in, but you're here all the same." Sassara had come by the ICU one day, and he and Lauren spent the better part of the morning talking and walking around the hospital grounds with his dog.

"Charlie's a great listener, he's really honest and kind," Lauren says. "I'm comforted by knowing that there is this one other person out there who can fathom exactly what I've been through, because he has been through it too. I've really needed that person."

Stevenson offered everything he could, too. "He was concerned, warm, and helpful without being too pushy," Lauren remembers. Stevenson and his wife had John, Alissa, and Lauren over for dinner one night. "It was the first time I'd been able to put the worry and stress out of my mind for any amount of time," Lauren says. "The first time I'd felt a little bit normal in the week since we'd been back in town."

Those terrible hours on the ledge, everyone was realizing, had just been the beginning. Emmett's predicament lacked the suddenness of a death in the mountains or the relief of a successful rescue with a minor injury, and his purgatory in Providence affected everyone who went to visit. With Emmett in limbo, visitors didn't have to imagine what it would be like for a mountain tragedy to tear across a family. They could see it.

"The thing that haunted me most about it was that—any number of times—it could have been *me*," Stevenson says. "Obviously, accidents happen. And a lot of times, they're just reported in one or two sentences. Sometimes you have heard of the people, but oftentimes not. But to be in that hospital room, to see the grief of the people who were with Emmett and their families? It was pretty daunting."

Though they worried for Emmett above anything else, John and Alissa grew nervous for Lauren. "Anchorage was a little tough—we felt for Lauren, navigating this by herself," Alissa says. "When we were there, I slept in the same bed with her every night. I was always with her." While grateful for the comfort of her friends, being surrounded by Emmett's family seemed to overwhelm Lauren. Everyone needed space and time in order to process what had happened—and what was still happening with Emmett.

A few days after the team landed in Anchorage, Zerkel offered to have John, Alissa, and Lauren tour Elmendorf in order to meet some of the rescuers involved in the mission, including Brister, Breun, Ercolani, and Guedea.

In the Hidden Mountains, when Brister and John had first met during the rescue, they'd been forced to trust each other in a split second. The moment Brister saw John at Elmendorf, he wrapped him in a massive bear hug.

"You know, a lot of times we rescue people and we don't know if they lived or died," Breun tells me.

"This civil search and rescue is extremely rewarding, but it's also very stressful. As a squadron, we're constantly figuring out how to best take care of our people," Ercolani, who has been flying civil and combat rescues for seventeen years, explains. "It takes an emotional and physical toll on you. . . . There's not really a book written for how to do this. We have to look out for each other."

Like other SAR groups in the country, the 176th is making a concerted effort to reach out to those rescued to better close this psychological loop, according to Ercolani. "A lot of times we do these missions, it's this person's worst day," he says. Following up "may be therapeutic to *you*, but it's *extremely* therapeutic to the person you rescued. Especially in the more traumatic instances."

Over the following weeks, Brister and a few of the other PJs paid visits to Emmett in Providence. They reported on Emmett's condition to the other rescuers and spent time with his family.

John and Alissa ended up staying in Anchorage for about a week after the rescue. Alissa had to resume sorting through her father's affairs. Tasked with finding care for Emmett when—and if—he got out of Providence, Alissa also set up a GoFundMe page to pay for his increasing medical care. Though some of the rescue was covered by insurance, the costs were mounting. GoFundMe had become a sad necessity in climbing accidents, filling financial gaps where insurance would not.

Before they left Anchorage, John and Alissa sat with Emmett as he lay in the hospital bed. His head was misshapen, oblong after his recent surgery, a soft spot left where Rosenbaum had removed part of his skull. Although Emmett was not conscious, John took out his iPhone and put on a song, a little tin-whistle ditty the musician and climber Sean Villanueva O'Driscoll had recorded on one of his expeditions, a spoof shanty replete with a mandolin. Emmett loved live music, and he loved this song so much he'd made it the ringtone on his cell phone. John and Alissa watched, hoping something would happen.

Suddenly, they realized Emmett was bobbing his head to the beat. It was slight, barely noticeable, but it was the first sign that part of him was still in there.

"If you had seen where he was and what happened to him and what he looked like," Breun says, "you'd be amazed he even lived."

# NINETEEN

My wife, Alexa, and I had spent plenty of wonderful days in the mountains, but we'd never had the nerve to go on a real alpine trip together. I'd always dreamed of taking her to Alaska, cutting her loose on that terrain, watching with a dash of awe and pride, as I usually did when she climbed. I wondered if she would like it there, if she would fall in love with Alaska the same way I had. I'd dreamed of watching her eyes widen as a glacier plane landed and she comprehended the sheer magnitude of the place.

When we met, Alexa and I were both obsessive climbers, logging at least three or four days a week to train or climb. She'd just moved to North Conway, New Hampshire, and she came to a party we hosted in the flophouse I rented with a few other climbing bums. I had built a crack climbing machine (two sixteen-foot two-by-eights connected with washers and threaded rod, which you could adjust to different widths in order to practice crack climbing) and lashed it to a tree in our backyard. We'd grunt our way up until the thing filled our hands with kiln-dried splinters or ejected us into the humid New England air. At twenty-five, my love life felt just as insecure: only a matter of time until I was ejected.

That night, I kept staring at this tall, angular girl I'd never seen before, the embers of the bonfire lighting her features against surrounding darkness. Suddenly, breaking my reverie, she was up on the crack machine, like a spark shot out of the fire. I had no idea she climbed. But as she waltzed up with ease, my hubristic crush morphed into amazement. When I stared at her feet and realized she was wearing sandals, this amazement turned swiftly into nausea. How was she enduring something so painful with such a smile on her face? This woman, I thought to myself, was a hell of a climber. She reversed her movements after reaching the top and then she receded back into the shadows, ignoring the gobsmacked onlookers as if her compulsion to climb was something to be ashamed of.

All that autumn, too chicken to ask her to climb and *definitely* too scared to ask her out on a date, I kept bumbling my way through awkward conversations at parties. By winter, she'd moved into a room in the house we rented. I remained too afraid to ask her out on a date. But eventually, bumbling aside, one thing led to another.

Alexa cared about vertical movement more than anybody I knew. She didn't want to go to movies or idle around, didn't need to hunt for the perfect espresso like I did. Now I didn't have to explain why I left for months at a time or missed social occasions; I didn't have to agonize about spending time with my partner when the ice conditions were good. Climbing—and nothing else—mattered. We spent months on trips, chasing ephemeral ice routes or Yosemite granite, cultivating small sponsorships.

Climbing together always strengthened our relationship. When we'd started dating, Alexa was a far stronger rock climber, having grown up competing in gyms and sport climbing around the country, but I could put my head down to grind out scary, icy pitches in the mountains pretty well. On our best days, we'd put this all together. Climbing reminded us that our conflicting temperaments and personalities could dovetail, could create something greater than the sum of its parts.

Still, when the two of us roped up, I exuded a degree of caution I'd never afforded my other climbing partners. When she returned late from an ice climb with other friends I'd fret, try not to look at my phone, realizing how it felt to be on the receiving end when I was away on expeditions.

As we went through the things couples invariably go through, we found climbing wasn't everything. But we knew we'd *always* climb together; those moments remained the finest of our relationship. I loved seeing Alexa's green eyes sparkling out from the folds of her down jacket at a belay, and watching her shyness transform into a kind of grace as she danced up a trad climb or a tricky column of ice. I still do.

I knew I could not fathom the moments Lauren must have gone through on her belay ledge, in part because I'd imagined them so much, wondering what I would have done in her shoes if the person I loved was up there instead. It could have been me, or Alexa, or any of us.

By chance, that week, eleven days after Emmett's rescue, I'd be heading to Anchorage to work for a month. The Robertses requested I check in with Lauren while I was there.

"Do they know what his injuries are?" Alexa asked before I left for Alaska. I checked an e-mail David had sent me.

"C5 and C6. What does that mean?" My brain didn't compute, but Alexa, slogging through nursing school at the time, decoded this instantly.

"It means he's paralyzed."

IN ANCHORAGE, I GOT IN TOUCH WITH LAUREN BY WAY OF ALISSA. Was there anything Lauren needed, I asked? *Distraction.*

Instinctively, I suggested to Lauren that we meet at the

Anchorage Rock Gym. Not until after she agreed did I realize climbing—which governed so much of my own social life—might be triggering for her.

We worked our way through the brightly taped boulder problems. At this time, I knew very little about the rescue or Emmett's current state. At one point, Lauren sat on the bouldering mat, talking about their relationship. She laughed remembering him trying to teach her how to ski and helping her down the bunny slope despite his ability at the sport. Then she stopped and looked down at the floor, perhaps realizing he'd never ski again.

Would she ever want to climb outside of a gym again? I wasn't sure. I'd always imagined myself to be a good listener, but in reality I felt awkward in this moment, unsure how to talk to her about these things.

Afterward we grabbed a beer at a local brewpub and kept the conversation focused on neutral subjects. I tried to make her laugh. I did impressions of my dad, whom Lauren had met a few times. I confided that I, too, struggled—often for hours—to come up with grammatically correct e-mails to send to David Roberts. Dumb humor was the best I could muster.

Lauren and Emmett had been together for three years. She was thirty-seven; he was forty. Did they think they'd be together forever? Everything had changed now.

Another friend had lost a sister in a freak trail-running accident that week. All of a sudden, none of these sports felt worth it. Biking back alone to Airport Heights, the neighborhood where I was staying, I tried to streak across the park's rail trail as quickly as possible, trying to feel little except the chilly summer air for a second. It didn't feel fast enough.

Emmett's accident resonated with me more than other accidents had. I hadn't known Lauren or Emmett at all, really. Plenty of friends of friends or acquaintances had had far worse happen to them in the mountains. Yet somehow—probably because Lauren and Emmett had been a couple—Emmett's fall hit me in the gut more than hearing about well-known climbers who were killed. Emmett and Lauren were so *normal*. How could this sport have done this to them?

EMMETT WAS DREAMING OF CITIES. ONE REMINDED HIM OF ISTAN-bul, which he loved, but it wasn't. He was trying to find something, or trying to escape, but he couldn't. He'd be broke, sleeping under bridges by the river. Then the sequence would shift and he'd be hunting for water: for him, for a whole group of people. He'd be stuck in a room made of stitched-together skin and would need to claw his way out. This thread of confinement strung his dreams together. He felt trapped, even in his subconscious.

Every once in a while, an incessant beeping would penetrate the murk. Then he'd lose consciousness again, go back to the dreams, and come to again a little later.

He'd been given a tracheostomy in order to suck out the fluid that was building in his lungs, so a tube snaked down his throat. He'd had emergency brain surgery, then once he was stable enough, he'd had another surgery to fuse his spine. Dr. Rosenbaum had prioritized Emmett's brain over his other injuries, because this was the most pressing threat to Emmett's life. Still, no one knew how much cognitive function he would regain.

"I mean, I can't really remember exactly when I realized he was still Emmett," Dora says. "I don't know how many weeks went by. He couldn't talk because of the tubes. But in that time period, just from the questions we were asking and how he would respond, I got the feeling he was going to be okay."

To Emmett, experiencing this all trapped inside the ICU with IVs and tubes and unable to move, coming around was piecemeal and terrifying. Sometimes there would be faces he knew: his parents, Jessi. John and Alissa. Lauren. All he knew was that he was hurt, but he had little notion of the severity of his injuries; he felt as if he'd broken his legs or something but would soon be better. He faded in and out of wakefulness. One night, when Emmett's visitors had gone home, he lay immobile, trying to summon a nurse in the hallway, but he couldn't move his body. He couldn't speak. A machine beeped in staccato rhythm.

"I lay there for hours, gasping, trying to say 'Help.' At that point I still had a hole in my throat," he remembers. "I would sit there mouthing. I couldn't really move my arms much at the time so I would kind of be moving them around a little, but nobody was responding. But I'd look through the window and see nurses walking around and I'd stare at them, hoping they'd lock eyes with me and come in, but nobody did." The feeling of being trapped in his own body was one of utter isolation, and in the morning, he communicated to Lauren how terrified it made him. From that night on, Lauren organized a rotating schedule of guests, making sure Emmett never spent the night alone.

# TWENTY

Climbers tend to be goal oriented, always fixated on new challenges and meticulous self-improvement. They are either dogged from the get-go or this trait is hammered into them by the sport itself if they stick with it for long enough. High-level sport climbers fall on a route hundreds of times, succeeding only once, the small shifting of how they grab a hold or the slightest tweak in training or nutrition providing that sliver of difference. Hard work pays off.

The expectation with a devastating injury, then, is that with hard work or a can-do attitude, a person may recover. Or that platitudes like "This is your new mountain to climb" can be slung at the problem, as if it would go away—as if a spinal cord injury is another equation that can be solved by the mental arithmetic climbers employ to move upward on rock or ice. Effort and grit garners results.

But quadriplegia is bound by rules and laws over which humans have no control. The injury remains absolute.

When most cells die, they regenerate. But nearly all neurons lack this vital ability. The neurons in the spinal cord look like jellyfish, with tails (called axons) that run down the spine. The spinal cord itself acts like a subway tunnel, transmitting information to and from the brain via these long, slinking axons that are bundled into the spinal cord—not unlike the hundreds of nylon fibers that make up a climbing rope. Axons receive information in an instant. They are the reason we know to quickly take our hand off a hot stove. But if axons are severed in a spinal cord injury, they cannot grow back. And depending on where the break happens, different parts of the body are subsequently cut off from this information being fed to and from the brain.

A person whose spinal cord is severed in their lower back—like a T, for thoracic vertebra, region—typically loses the use of their legs. But higher up the spine, paralysis grows more consequential. In Emmett's case, his C6 (C for cervical) cut off neurological communication between his brain and nearly everything from his sternum down. He could move his biceps and triceps and wrists, but not his thumbs or fingers.

Before World War I, patients with spinal cord injuries often died from complications shortly after their initial injuries occurred. But when the modern weaponry of the Great War shattered the bodies of tens of thousands of soldiers en masse, medical workers began a concerted effort to better manage broken spinal cords. Of these soldiers, D. T. Max writes in *The New Yorker*, "eighty per cent died in short order from sepsis initiated by bedsores or kidney infections, and many of the survivors died soon after. . . . Amid so much carnage, it came as a revelation that simple protocols—always using a catheter to remove urine, turning a patient in bed every few hours—increased life expectancy dramatically."

The human body is not meant to endure such a shock. And historically, it hasn't. Even today, these same side effects often kill spinal cord injury (SCI) patients. Bed and pressure sores, sepsis, and pneumonia, all of which harangue an already compromised immune system, eventually take their toll, often on patients who are over fifty.

SCI research is driven mostly by public interest and, therefore, by funding. Because so little is still known about how to repair the axons in the spinal cord, SCI research is a difficult bet for investors looking to back the next miracle pharmaceutical technology or high-tech lab. The aha moment still seems to be very far off. Though the crux is simple—creating, replacing, or regrowing the damaged axons—this problem has presented an insurmountable obstacle for spinal cord researchers over the past century.

In 2000, a neuroscientist in Madrid revealed she had been able to sever the spinal cords of rats in her lab and get them to walk again by giving them transplants of olfactory ensheathing cells (OECs), which are found in the mucous membrane of the nasal cavity. These are neurons with a key distinction separating them from the neurons in the spinal cord: They can regenerate. By introducing the OECs into the lab rats' spinal cords, the scientist was able to regenerate movement in rats with completely severed spinal cords.

Quickly, doctors in China and Portugal began offering a similar transplant option for human patients. But "these weren't clinical trials. These were untested-in-humans treatments, with no guarantees of anything," Kate Willette says in her guide to SCI, *Don't Call It a Miracle*. One doctor in China even reported a wait list for his treatment of more than six thousand patients.

Despite the thousands of hopeful applicants, there has been only one case of an OEC transplant actually working in a human. In 2010, a Polish carpenter and volunteer firefighter named Darek Fidyka was asleep at home next to his girlfriend, Justyna, when he was awakened by the sound of his Volkswagen being smashed in. It was Justyna's ex-husband, who had gone to prison for beating Justyna and had a history of alcoholism. When Fidyka walked outside to try and calm Jaroslaw down, Jaroslaw stabbed him eighteen times. The knife cut his spinal cord at the T9 vertebrae, paralyzing him from the waist down.

Because SCI patients can sometimes regain functionality on their own through physical therapy, and because this often occurs in the first several months after an injury, Fidyka was asked to undergo twenty-one months of vigorous PT first. Then, in 2012, a team led by the late British neuroscientist Dr. Geoffrey Raisman operated on Fidyka, removing OECs from Fidyka's nasal cavity. "The surgeons didn't just inject his OECs into his cord; instead, they harvested four tiny strips of nerve tissue (meaning, bundles of axons) from one of his ankles. Those four strips were placed across the hole in his cord, where they would hopefully form a sort of bridge upon which the OECs could guide the axons to grow," Willette writes.

By 2014, Fidyka was able to walk with the help of canes. For all intents and purposes, Raisman's surgery had been a success. "To me, this is more impressive than a man walking on the Moon. I believe this is the moment when paralysis can be reversed," Raisman told a BBC film crew in 2014. In the attempt to cure SCI, as Max puts it, "Ensheathing cells have become a surprise contender."

Scientists have also begun experimenting with e-stim—inserting an electronic stimulator to sit on the broken neurons and mimic brain signals with an electronic current, which has allowed some patients with broken backs to regain motor function in their legs. While e-stim and OEC transplants offer glimpses of what may someday be achieved, neither offers the silver bullet to curing SCI—not yet, at least.

"The issue, not surprisingly, is finding the money to make all [this] happen. Normally when new drugs or devices come on the market, it's because they hit a stage of development where some company can see profit on the horizon. That's hard to achieve with the stimulators, precisely because actually restoring function after paralysis is such uncharted territory," says Willette.

Fidyka's story was remarkable, but hardly the norm for patients who have suffered a spinal cord injury. Climbers are accustomed to training their bodies and their minds and achieving acute feedback in performance; like any sport, there's a direct correlation between time and effort and a bump in performance. But paralysis doesn't allow room for feedback like that. It's the neurological equivalent of running into a brick wall.

ON JULY 30TH, MORE THAN A MONTH AFTER THE RESCUE, EMMETT was finally stable enough to be moved. The swelling had receded in his brain and his skull had been reattached, but he still couldn't move on his own. Attendants wheeled him onto the runway at Ted Stevens Anchorage International Airport strapped to a yellow gurney. They transitioned him onto the plane. Lauren accompanied him, along with three medical personnel.

After a forced landing in the Midwest due to thunderstorms, the plane touched down at Hanscom Air Force Base in Bedford, Massachusetts, in the early-morning hours of July 31st. An ambulance took Emmett to the neuropathy intensive care unit at Massachusetts General Hospital, where he remained for another week. As Emmett's family grappled with the more immediate and overwhelming aftermath of his accident, John and Alissa had offered to spearhead finding the best spot for Emmett's recovery. Weighing the options, they'd decided that Spaulding Rehabilitation Center in Charlestown, Massachusetts, within striking distance of the family and friends Emmett would need to rely on more than ever, would offer the best and healthiest care after he left the intensive care unit.

Emmett has no memory of being told the extent of his injuries while in Anchorage. During his discharge from Mass General, however, a doctor informed him he'd lost function in most of his body. This news shocked him. For someone with Emmett's boundless optimism, the statement didn't even compute. Who the hell was she to tell him he'd never walk again?

"I think I may have questioned her: *Are you sure?* After that I got upset at her. I told myself, 'That's not good bedside manner.' Why would she steal my hope away? I started blaming her for giving me a bad diagnosis that obviously wasn't correct. But at that point, I still wasn't moving. I couldn't use my arms. I was still so beat up that I couldn't prove her wrong."

Spaulding's Charlestown campus is a shimmering, modern facility abutting the Atlantic Ocean. A patient can look out over Boston Harbor or watch airliners rattle overhead upon leaving Logan International Airport. It is the official teaching center for the Harvard Medical School Department of Physical Medicine and Rehabilitation, and it is considered one of the finest physical rehabilitation centers in the world. For a new quadriplegic, few better places existed to begin therapy.

"Physical therapy is not meant to be watched," Max wrote in his piece about SCI. "It is intimate and awkward, the gap between the well and the diminished underscored at every moment."

It was hard to tell what was more difficult: the act of trying to get his body prepared for even routine tasks, like sitting or rolling over in bed, or the oppressive knowledge of his quadriplegia, which he'd been spared from in Anchorage. For the first two weeks of his inpatient treatment, Emmett denied the permanence of his injury. He'd concoct excuses—a cast still covered his arm, and *that* was why he couldn't use either of them. He tried to show up his caregivers. They were just wrong about him. But he couldn't prove anything: He couldn't move.

Fidyka had remained conscious during his attack and he'd *felt* the axons in his spinal cord die. "I can remember very vividly losing feeling in my legs, bit by bit," he told Max in an interview. "It started in the upper part of the spine and was moving slowly while

I lay waiting for the ambulance to arrive." Emmett, who had been unconscious during the rescue, now struggled to contextualize his new reality, toggling between optimism and despair. If the actual physical therapy was difficult, the knowledge of how little it was achieving was a tougher pill to swallow. Emmett would be stood up with help from assistants or work on moving his neck from left to right. "That's not progress," he says. "You can't call that progress."

Emmett *had* made remarkable progress in recovering from his TBI, however—beyond what anyone's expectations were. In and out of consciousness and with a trach tube in Alaska, the improvements weren't perceptible. But as what could heal on his body healed, his memory and cognitive function returned mostly intact, apart from the hour leading up to the accident, of which he still has no recollection. Emmett has no memory of what caused his thirty-foot fall while he was out of sight of Lauren, John, and Alissa, and no one will ever know what happened with any certainty. Perhaps he'd been hit on the head by a falling rock. Perhaps he'd stepped or pulled on a block that gave way.

Whatever the cause of the fall, it's possible that a surprising aspect of the hours that immediately followed had an impact on his potential for recovery. Artificially inducing hypothermia has become the standard of care for medical staff dealing with cardiac arrest, as hypothermia slows the heart and breathing. The body thus places less demand on vital organs. Studies have suggested that "therapeutic" hypothermia induced in adult TBI patients may slow the buildup of intracranial pressure that damages the brain. Emmett, in and out of consciousness on the ledge for nine hours in wet weather with temperatures hovering just above freezing, was certainly hypothermic. Ironically, the condition that kills so many outdoor adventurers may have contributed to saving his mind.

In August, David and Sharon came to visit Emmett at Spaulding. David wasn't sure how it would go. Would Emmett hate him?

David was still struggling with his own guilt after their expedition. The "fuckups" he'd castigated in his *Alpinist* article for relying on communication devices for rescue had been hypothetical, but Emmett and the team were close friends. In a lot of ways, Emmett reminded him of Ed Bernd, Roberts's climbing partner who had fallen to his death on Mount Huntington. In both cases, it was Roberts's optimism that had shepherded the climbers to Alaska.

"Of all the people I was going to meet when I got back to Boston," Emmett told him during that visit, "I dreaded meeting you the most."

"Why?"

"Because you did all these expeditions and you never fucked up. And I fucked up on my first one," Emmett replied. Both of them broke down.

"That wrenched me," Roberts told me. "That's where my guilt comes in. I pushed them really hard."

Most difficult, perhaps, was Emmett and Lauren's realization that normality would forever elude them. Overwhelmed, Lauren tried to forge Emmett's new necessities into their day-to-day reality. They'd been together for three years; they weren't married, and technically, medical decisions were initially up to Emmett's parents, with whom she sometimes disagreed. For the month Emmett remained in inpatient therapy, Lauren scheduled a series of supporters to stay with him during the night, so he'd never feel the abandonment he had experienced upon waking in Anchorage. But spending the night in Spaulding and rushing off to work the next day was a tall order for Emmett's friends, who were mostly working professionals. John and Alissa were still working at the time, while also trying to consolidate their things and prepare for hitting the road. Alissa remembers trying to catch some shut-eye on a teeny love seat in Emmett's hospital room before donning a suit and giving a presentation to her entire company the next morning.

"They'd roll Emmett over three times during the middle of the night," John says. "And they weren't quiet about any of it." From a purely physical standpoint, the schedule wore everyone down.

"I wonder if Emmett is even aware of it," Emily says. "His family was staying in places and shuttling rides and we were rotating sleeping in the hospital with Emmett every night: When he was in Spaulding, there was one of us staying with him every single night."

This new world Lauren and Emmett faced was painful and exhausting. Their third-floor apartment in Somerville was no longer an option, so Lauren found a new apartment a stone's throw from Spaulding. She recruited a score of friends to schlepp all their furniture to the new place in order to prepare it for Emmett's homecoming.

Emmett had a two-week lag time between his inpatient and outpatient physical therapy. It was during this time the couple realized just how difficult life was going to be, if they'd had any disillusionment before. Emmett needed a mechanical hoist to get him into the shower. He needed to be rolled over constantly to avoid pressure sores. His insurance covered a mechanical wheelchair because Emmett couldn't push his own, though he'd regained control over his biceps and triceps.

Lauren must have been struggling inwardly. Her needs—distance and time to reflect—stood in opposition to the requirements of the friend and family network that made Emmett's life possible in those months. "It's not so traumatic and dramatic to me as it is to her," Emmett notes now. Lauren had suffered through minute by minute, hour by hour, alone on the ledge, while Emmett had no memory of that time. She didn't want to relive the accident, but Emmett desperately wanted to know what had happened to him and why he'd fallen. Lauren hadn't seen the accident, so there was no way to know with any certainty. "She would break down crying pretty quickly. I kind of got out of the habit of asking her."

To John and Alissa, it was as if Lauren split into two separate people. When Emmett's friends would swing by the apartment or his parents would visit, she'd sequester herself in another room. But she'd emerge if a mutual friend like John or Alissa stopped by, the same old Lauren again.

Alissa looks back on that summer as psychological warfare. She'd just lost her father and sorted through his possessions. The trip to the Hidden Mountains, intended to launch the road trip she and John had long dreamed of, had gravely injured one of their best friends. Both felt as if they needed to be there for Emmett, but their lease was up and they had given notice at their jobs. Like it or not, they were committed to leaving Boston. The timing couldn't have been worse.

"We definitely felt in some ways that we were abandoning Emmett," John says.

The couple experienced different reactions to Emmett's injuries, too. Although both remained obsessed with climbing, Alissa decided she'd had enough of alpine climbing for the time being.

"John very much excels in that terrain," Alissa muses. "I think he probably accepts the outcome of our trip as one you know is possible. For me, after seeing Emmett's fall firsthand, it doesn't feel like it's worth it to me. A lot of that is not just the accident itself but how it affects the community around you, and your family, and your friends."

Instead of going to Patagonia as planned, they decided to stick to more controllable rock climbing objectives. By the end of summer, they'd loaded their van and headed west, promising to visit Emmett whenever they could.

The November after Emmett's fall, a local gear store held a fundraiser in Boston to help pay for his medical bills. The place was packed. John had taken time out from his traveling to come back for the week. The retail outlet was stacked with sleek $700 jackets and pants. The walls were plastered with photographs of honed models, all wind-blown hair and perfectly manicured stubble, ice and rock climbing in flawless outfits. Background music coursed through speakers, a tap flowed with free beer. For a medical fundraiser, it felt pretty darn hip.

Alexa and I showed up with my dad, driving down from North Conway. At the door, we met the Robertses and filtered in from the sleet. It was the first time I'd seen Emmett since the accident. Lauren stood behind his wheelchair, greeting everybody as they came in. When she saw our little party, she shed a few tears before quickly wiping them away, composing herself, hugging everyone. The last time I had seen her had been in Anchorage.

The store manager got up and gave his two cents. "I don't want to live in a community where we don't catch those who fall!" He flashed a grin, absorbing the spotlight for a second before introducing the main speaker. After the show, we elbowed through the crowd for a while, saying hi to people we recognized from crags and ice festivals. It was reassuring to see everyone come out for something like this.

A few beers later we filtered out again into the Boston sleet, and then we were gone—same as everybody. It was over.

"There's a reality that as much as the community loved me and wanted to be supportive of me, and really wanted to be there for me and cared deeply for me, it's still a *climbing* community," Emmett tells me. "The accident happened and there was this huge outpouring of support. And everybody cared, and everybody— truthfully and honestly, from the deepest part of their souls— came out to support me and prove to me that they loved me and cared about what happened. But it was also a single event. It ended there. There's no continuation of that, it's not perennial anymore. It's over now. My participation in the climbing community, it's over."

In rehab, Emmett's cohorts were men and women who'd gotten their injuries in car accidents or falling off ladders, and who could not relate to losing the tight-knit camaraderie of a sport like climbing. "There's no drunk-driving-into-a-tree community," he points out. Losing his place in this world felt almost as hard as losing the function in his body. "It's not the fault of the community. It's just that we have nothing to talk about. We never talked about anything besides climbing before; why should we now?"

IN 1997, THE WELSH CLIMBER AND WRITER PAUL PRITCHARD WON the Boardman Tasker Award for Mountain Literature for his book *Deep Play*, an examination of a life lived in pursuit of the most difficult climbs in the world. He and his then-girlfriend, a professional climber named Celia Bull, took the earnings and hit the road on a yearlong around-the-globe adventure.

In Tasmania, Pritchard and Bull decided to attempt a feature called the Totem Pole, a striking tower of rock that rose out of the Pacific Ocean, eroded by time and weather until it created a slender monolith jutting out of the ocean. To the pair, making a free ascent was irresistible.

Pritchard was one of the best rock climbers in the world. He'd made a career out of climbing what others could not: terrifying lines on crumbling slate in Wales, routes plagued by constant storms in Torres del Paine. Plenty of people possess the technical chops to climb hard routes, and plenty of people are brave, but the cross section of climbers who possess both traits is rare indeed. Pritchard was the poster boy for these bold, runout climbs.

He'd taken two bad falls in his career: one at Gogarth, in northern Wales, and one on Ben Nevis, the highest mountain in the British Isles and a classic winter destination for Scottish and British climbers. If these two falls felt like a common side effect of pushing the limits of his sport, Pritchard's accident on the Totem Pole was nothing short of random, a fluke occurrence.

Despite the Totem Pole's short height—it's just two pitches—it's such a striking feature that climbers travel from all over the world to make an ascent. All previous parties except for one had aid climbing up the slender tower; Pritchard and Bull, in contrast, were angling for the second free ascent. In order to reach the Totem Pole, they crossed a horizontal line called a Tyrolean traverse, which ran high above the water to the summit, and rappelled in. As Pritchard reached the bottom, the tide threw waves onto his rock shoes and chalk bag, and he called to Celia to stop at the second belay station halfway up the face so she wouldn't get similarly drenched. Bull rappelled to an anchor partway up, and Pritchard prepared to ascend the rope to join her. "I didn't see any loose rock on the Totem Pole," Pritchard tells me. "It's the most wave-blasted rock in Christendom. But there was obviously one loose flake."

As Pritchard weighted the rope, it snagged over this single loose rock and dislodged it. He didn't hear it as it sailed through the air. The missile hit him straight in the head.

"When I regained consciousness, I was upside down, confused and there was blood pissing out of my head," Pritchard writes in *The Totem Pole*, his book about the accident that would change his life.

"It was completely random. There was no way I could have foreseen that," Pritchard told me.

It took a while for Bull to register what had happened. She recounts the moment on the British podcast *40 for Tea*: "I just heard the rockfall. And then nothing. You're just holding your breath. . . . You know what you're supposed to do. And you can't believe it's happening. I think I talked my way through it. And just going, 'Calm down, just breathe, breathe.' I was shouting to him: 'You've got to help me.'"

Bull ascended back to the top of the Totem Pole and set up

a haul system, pulling Pritchard upward with a small mechanical advantage—usually a feat done by six or twelve rescuers operating in shifts—and secured him to a ledge. She sprinted back to try and find more help, and soon a Tasmanian rescue team was en route.

The ensuing brain injury changed Pritchard's life. He lost much of the function in the left side of his body. He suffered lapses in memory, his personality changed. "I had no idea what a brain injury entailed at that point," Pritchard explains. The next year was spent making small recoveries, from hospitals and rehab centers, in both Tasmania and his native Wales.

"I sold all my climbing gear," he says. "I thought I would never go climbing again. After about nine months I put it all up for sale. I just sold the lot of it. I remember crying. One of the reasons I ultimately moved to Tasmania out of Llanberis was because I didn't feel part of the community anymore. All these people were doing really physical things around me and I was still in a wheelchair. I got really depressed about seeing all these people, all these physical people all the time. I wanted to escape and find a more cerebral community . . . straightaway I went to university and got involved in the artist and writing scene quite a lot."

Soon after the Totem Pole, Bull quit climbing, too, and fell into sailing. Several months after the accident, she told him she no longer wanted to be his girlfriend.

"A big day," Pritchard wrote in *The Totem Pole*. "The woman I love decided it would be best if we didn't see each other again on a romantic level. In other words she has left me. She broke the news in the van whilst bringing me back from the hospital. She parked up in a lay-by because she couldn't see through the tears."

Pritchard is circumspect about what happened between him and Bull. The pair have remained very close. "There were a lot of good memories tied up in those six years of togetherness. And the fact that she saved my life must surely mean I am eternally indebted

to her." She is still one of his closest friends. "The dynamic completely changed. . . . When the accident happened, I think I was
just so dependent on her for everything. Celia couldn't sustain that
level of dependence. And that's not to denigrate her at all."

When Lauren and Emmett returned to Boston, David Roberts
recommended they read *The Totem Pole*. Emmett couldn't find an
audiobook version and could no longer read a physical book, but
Lauren sat down and worked her way through a copy. Pritchard
and Bull's story was the closest thing to a guide Lauren had to
understanding her unique position, according to Emmett. "I think
it really helped her understand the trauma she was going through.
It helped her justify and recognize it: This is not her being broken,
as much as a normal reaction that any partner would go through in
this type of situation.

"When Lauren started to contextualize what she was going
through and she tried to explain it to me, I like to think I was open
to that. I did my best to put myself in her shoes and understand it. I
know I tried awfully hard to be supportive of her. And often talked
about how the injury was so much worse for her than it was for me.
But you know, that's lip service, when I'm asking her to provide
care for me. I can be as sympathetic as I can to what she's going
through, but at the same time I'm also demanding: 'Hey, I need you
to do this, I need you to do that.'"

There was no real template for any of this. Insurance wouldn't
cover a full-time caregiver, and Lauren struggled to fill that role
and still work. "She was exhausted," Jessi remembers. Emmett relied on Lauren in every imaginable way. As much as he wanted to
reciprocate the support, he was physically incapable of doing so.
"How can you not use your hands?" Jessi says. "I can't even imagine
how frustrating that is."

"Lauren was really distraught. You could see it every day. She
was really struggling," Emmett tells me. "She was very unhappy,

very distraught, and she cried a lot. She spent a lot of time trying to do other things but you could tell they weren't quite bringing her the same satisfaction she was hoping they would. She'd go on climbing trips. When she got back I'd be excited, ask her what she did, but she was never quite as excited as I hoped she'd be."

Lauren even flew out to climb with John and Alissa a few times when they were on the road, and she still climbed in the gym and around New England, but the sport had taken on an entirely different character for her. It could not be the same as it was before. The couple did a few therapy sessions in the spring of 2019. Looking back on them, Emmett feels as if he entered with an open mind, though sometimes the situation made him angry or bitter. How could he provide emotional support when he couldn't take care of himself? That spring he was once again bedridden—the result of a surgery to remove a pressure sore—for four months.

"I feel like I went into those discussions thinking we need to fix whatever is going wrong for Lauren, because she is struggling so hard." But at the same time, that solution felt unfair. "I'm just surviving here, day-to-day," he'd tell himself, growing resentful.

In May, eleven months after the accident, Lauren told Emmett she could no longer maintain their relationship. This devastated him. It devastated them both. "I cried a lot," Emmett says. "I think I cried for about a month.

"Although we hadn't talked about getting married or having kids or anything, I think it was implicit that that was the direction we were headed. But also, she had become my de facto caregiver. . . . She was just the rock. She was the rock that was by my side the whole time, you know? To lose that rock all of a sudden—I felt like I was set adrift."

Each time I speak to Lauren, she's fearful of how she'll be portrayed during the events after Emmett's rescue. Ultimately, and understandably, she is unwilling to speak about most of the things that happened after Emmett was flown off the ledge in the Hidden Mountains. But perhaps her fear says more about the outdoor community or our expectations of what a spouse should do than it does about Lauren herself. Sadly, this stigma appears to hold especially for female survivors, for whom there is a societal expectation to remain ardent and steadfast in their care, even when the trauma of an accident has extended to them.

The split wrenched Emmett in a different way from the emotional gut punch he'd experienced during his breakup with Beth. This was something much deeper. From the moment the accident happened, he'd depended on Lauren for his survival. "I'll be honest. When she told me she was leaving, I thought it was all over. It felt as if there was no path forward—no way to be successful living without her. I was certain I would be put in a nursing home somewhere, that I couldn't find any other way for life to continue."

# TWENTY-ONE

In my twenties, for a distinct eight-year period, if you'd asked me if mountain climbing was worth the risk, I would have said yes. Soloing, when the stillness of my surroundings meshed with my own laser focus, stimulated me more than anything. Climbing alone demanded a hard, simple honesty and it provided moments of brilliant clarity in return. It didn't care if I was poor, if I'd failed to land a job, or if I'd been dumped. Soloing felt like a simple act in a complicated world: a potentially lethal form of decluttering.

I'd convinced myself, in my hubris or blind optimism, that focus learned from experience would keep me safer. I would listen to my own breathing, to the sounds my crampons made against ice or rock, to the feeling of an ice ax swung just so, a flick mastered after thousands of hours and thousands of placements. I'd relax my shoulders, arch my back to stare at the route ahead, breathe, let the inhalations wash over me and calm me, close my eyes, and pull up.

When I headed to the mountains, I used this shallow rationale like a security blanket. The more I climbed in dangerous terrain, I reasoned, and the more I acclimated my brain to that kind of dizzying exposure or objective danger, the better I'd get at making those decisions. This is one way to look at it; the other is to recognize that mathematical odds care not for skill or bravery: more time equals more danger.

Gradually, little things happened on my own climbs that convinced me I was not in such perfect control of my environment as I'd once thought: a slipped foot, a piece of ice fracturing around a placement I'd assumed was solid.

The autumn after Emmett's accident I attempted Mount Robson, in the Canadian Rockies, with four other climbers. We were two teams, planning on climbing independently of each other. My good friend Ryan and I climbed together often and I trusted him immensely. But our third team member, Scott, was an unknown. Although Ryan had climbed with him, I never had.

The route we angled for was on a feature called the Emperor Face, a seven-thousand-foot wall of limestone and ice twelve miles into the backcountry. It is one of the great prizes in North American climbing. It felt within my wheelhouse. I'd been training hard and climbing in the mountains a lot. I'd grilled Ryan about Scott before the trip. He was newer to the mountains. He was nice and I liked him, but that didn't change the fact that we'd never roped up and now were planning to on one of the biggest climbs of our lives.

The night before we drove to Mount Robson, I tossed and turned in my hotel room, terrified not of the route but of my new, unknown partner. In the morning, I was a sentence away from opting out entirely, but I packed my bags and tried to shut my brain up as we drove to the trailhead.

After six hours of hiking we rounded the corner and got a look at the Emperor Face, only to find the dry summer had melted the ice couloir we'd hoped to climb. Instead, we turned our attention to an easier route called the Emperor Ridge: still a long undertaking, but nowhere near as daunting. I exhaled.

On our second day of climbing, Scott took the lead, trying to ascend a chimney.

"I'll be up this in no time," Scott said.

"Don't say that," one of us replied. "Everyone always says that before they start up."

Sure enough, Scott's feet started skating around in his crampons. The pitch was harder and more dangerous than it'd looked from below. *He just jinxed himself,* I remember thinking.

Scott struggled to find gear placements, wriggling his way up the chimney and out of sight. We kept hearing grunts from the chimney. He sounded more and more desperate.

"Watch me," he yelled down. There was panic in his voice. He was out of sight now.

Then we heard him yell, a scream of terror and desperation and utter fear, and suddenly he was off. As if in slow motion, I watched his body ricochet down the chimney. He tumbled upside down, his ice axes, attached to his harness by bungees, pinging off the rock. His back hit the wall hard. It was all very still again. For what seemed like an eternity, Scott did not move or speak.

*Holy shit, it finally happened* was all I could think. *This is what happens when people die in the mountains.* I looked at Ryan, next to me at our belay. I looked down at my own hands, clamped on the taut rope.

We lowered Scott back down to the stance. He'd fallen about forty feet. Some of the gear he'd placed slid down the rope; it had yanked out when he'd fallen. We needed to get out of there. Shock was coursing through him. But Scott had grown up tough in northern Maine. He'd known the plodding terror of touring Afghan cities from the inside of an army Humvee. He was inexperienced with climbing but not with fear. In a split second, he'd learned more about mountain climbing than I ever wanted to know.

The five of us (our two friends had also opted for retreat) began rappelling what we could, soloing down the easy terrain when we could. Berg Lake, the bright blue feature that helps make Robson so alluring, taunted us from five thousand feet below. On our first rappel, I leaned back and a cam ripped out of the anchor. In twenty years of climbing I'd never had that happen before. *We need to keep our focus. We can't lose control.* I exhaled, took a few deep breaths, took it one step at a time. Ryan reset the cam and I kept going.

Each time we downclimbed without the rope on, we noticed Scott was barely holding it together. I made sure—selfishly—to be above him, so that if he fell again, tumbling down the gully, he wouldn't take me with him. Alexa and I had gotten engaged just a few days earlier. I wanted to get the fuck out of there. We realized Scott needed a rope to get down, even on the more moderate terrain. We rigged rappels slowly and carefully.

"Hey." Ryan stopped me at one belay stance, lowering his glacier glasses to look me in the eyes. It was the first we'd had a second to talk since Scott's fall. "Are you okay?"

I wasn't certain, but I said I was fine. Ryan and I *needed* to be fine. We were all going to get off this mountain no matter what. One step at a time.

As night fell we bivouacked again on a big, broad shelf, resting and rehydrating. Scott alternated between realizing how lucky he'd been and spurts of nervousness. The next morning, after another several hours of downclimbing and rappelling, we reached the stream at the base of Berg Lake, returning to the land of the living. We shucked our packs, tossed our crampons and harnesses and gloves in a heap, and sat for a while, giggling. We followed the azure-blue creek back to the parking lot in a euphoric haze. We couldn't believe we were here. I felt like an idiot for going up on Robson against my intuition.

That night, wolfing down burgers and guzzling beer at a brewpub in Jasper, I vowed to dial it back a little bit: I'd have to find that tricky medium between what I wanted to climb and how much risk I wanted to take. I still loved it—the moments when you forget everything except your partners and the world you were immersed in. But I wanted to stack the odds in my favor and climb safer routes.

I fell off the wagon a few more times, including on a trip to Taulliraju, a fortresslike peak in Peru's northern Cordillera Blanca. For two weeks, as we acclimatized and watched the mountain from our base camp, it had appeared so formidable. But when we rasped up the approach trail, stars glistening in the cold air, when we sank our ice axes into a mountain I'd hoarded photographs of since high school, when those lingering doubts receded and all that mattered were the few moves ahead of us, when all you had to do was not fall, it felt so worth it. Though we gasped for air, we laughed with joy, too.

We turned tail halfway up the peak after a big, broad snow-slope threatened to avalanche on us, two layers of snow grinding against each other in the thin air.

CLIMBING DOESN'T ATTRACT THE FRINGE AS MUCH AS IT USED TO. It's hard to imagine Henry Barber standing in line at the local bouldering gym with a protein smoothie. Competitions have come a long way since the one in Snowbird aired on CBS in 1988; in 2021, climbers from all over the world traveled to Tokyo to compete in the delayed 2020 Olympics. Today's climbers are honed machines, trained to perfection, and the results—on plastic or real rock—are incredible.

And on paper, climbing's not a risky endeavor. According to statistics released by the American Alpine Club (AAC) in their annual report, *Accidents in North American Climbing*, an average of twenty-six climbers die in the United States every year, based on numbers collected from 1990 to 2020. Because so many accidents go unreported, it's hard to know how accurate such statistics are. It's

also hard to tell how much more popular the sport is becoming—
but if the proliferation of climbing gyms is anything to go by, then
it stands to reason that climbing accidents are *decreasing* per capita.

This makes sense. Most newer climbers aren't attracted to risk
and adventure the way earlier ones were, instead choosing safer, more
accessible versions of the sport. Many only climb inside, and many
will top rope, boulder, or sport climb—versions of climbing that lack
the objective hazards of traditional mountaineering or ice climbing. In addition, organizations such as the AAC and the American
Mountain Guides Association are standardizing education that was
once only taught by word of mouth, from climber to climber.

Yet as climbing further enters the American mainstream, it's
important to address the risk and loss that—despite these encouraging numbers—remains inherent in all aspects of the sport. In
2017, Madaleine Sorkin was on a trip to the Wind River Mountain
Range in Wyoming when a climber she didn't know fell six hundred feet to his death on an adjacent peak. The deceased climber's
partner had watched the accident happen. Sorkin, one of the most
accomplished rock climbers in the United States, walked with the
bereaved partner out of the mountains. For years, climbers and
mountaineers had lived by "grin and bear it" credos to parse accidents in their sport. Something needed to change.

Sorkin and others had been mulling the idea of creating a specific place for dealing with grief and trauma in the mountains, and
she proposed starting the Climbing Grief Fund (CGF) to Phil
Powers, who was at the time the president of the AAC. Powers was
enthusiastic. Before long, the CGF created an extended network
of professionals, resources, grants, and online talks that dealt with
some of the risks inherent in climbing.

"The cultural shift is happening in such a notable way, towards
normalizing seeking out support," Sorkin tells me. "I think part of
grief work is to soften the edges of this subject and create spaces

for talking, sharing in community about one's experience." At the same time, she acknowledges that initiatives like the CGF are often stabs in the dark. It's a messy subject.

American climbers, hesitant to talk about trauma in general, have had few outlets historically. "We don't have that many traditions or rituals we can share to be in that space together," Sorkin says. I ask her if she was afraid an initiative that included the word "grief" in its title would turn off younger climbers. "I was just hellbent on starting it. We didn't know if anyone would be receptive, but felt that showing climbers talking about their experiences with loss was key," she says.

Sorkin remembers setting up a workshop during the inaugural year of CGF. "A total newbie climber came up to me. She had seen some of our videos, and it was really cool to hear from her. She had just started climbing, and she realized: Okay, so this is a part of it."

"The way I see it now," Pritchard says, "is that everybody takes risks all the time. Walking up the stairs is a risk. Crossing the road is a risk. There's just this range of risk all the time, throughout your life. . . . And you can't get away from that."

IN 2020, A MEMBER OF THE MIT OUTING CLUB WAS KILLED A HUNdred feet or so from the top of Cannon Cliff in New Hampshire, just a pitch away from where a Dartmouth student had been saved by a Black Hawk a year earlier.

The leader of the climbing party headed hard right two hundred feet from the top of Moby Grape, a popular and fun route for most aspiring New England climbers. On her traverse right, she placed several pieces of gear. She remembered thinking that one of the pieces was placed under a loose flake the size of a refrigerator, and that it was odd that grass and dirt was growing *under* this flake—ultimately a sign the entire, deadly block was detached.

After a hundred feet, she built a belay and waited for her partner to complete the traverse—but as he did, the block somehow became dislodged and cut his rope as it fell. He had enough time to yell "Oh, God." The words were simple and oozed with the climber's knowledge that these could be his last moments. He fell and was killed instantly on impact.

The leader began screaming for help and a few climbers above them rappelled down to see what was wrong. The fallen climber had gotten caught on a ledge.

In the morning, we hauled his body the two hundred feet to the top of the cliff. It took hours, and hours more for a procession of volunteers to hike down with the weight of it all. As we sat in the parking lot, a Fish and Game officer brought the lead climber over to us. Her voice was mechanical, hollowed out by a lack of sleep and shock. It wasn't clear if she and the dead climber were romantically involved, but my mind raced to Lauren and Emmett. How could it not? I'd considered Emmett to have been incredibly *unlucky*. But the finality of the climber's death—its violent suddenness—drove home what Emmett still had. Emmett's being still existed, despite its changed form. He and I had talked not long before this; he'd just been to his niece's birthday party. Emmett's impish sense of humor was still there, his pervasive self-deprecation. Lauren had helped to save Emmett's life.

The woman at the base of Cannon asked mechanical, technical questions. "Was the cam placed badly?" She was asking if the man's death was her fault.

"This had nothing to do with you," one of the older rescuers said. The words hovered in the clear, cold air for a minute. No one could think of anything to say besides that.

"I need to know everything," the woman said. "I need to know because I am going to have to live with this for the rest of my life."

# TWENTY-TWO

After an injury occurs, ten to twenty percent of spinal cord injury (SCI) patients do not survive long enough to make it to the hospital. Of those who do, eight percent who incur injuries to the cervical area, like Emmett did, die within the first year after their accidents. Those who keep living past this initial year still endure a mortality rate two or three times higher than average. Pulmonary complications like pneumonia rank as the highest cause of death for those living with SCI. Two separate long-term studies of patient mortality—one conducted in Great Britain and the other in the United States—listed suicide as the second-highest cause of death.

While Emmett underwent therapy at Spaulding, he'd been recovering from a multitude of serious injuries. "They only get a few people in there a year who have a brain injury and a spinal cord injury," Jessi says. "It's just not that common." Sidetracked by his TBI and other medical issues, Emmett had less opportunity to work on rehab in the initial phases of his recovery. Little things, like a mistake with what kind of pillow he'd prop himself up with, spiraled into insidious, long-term problems. A heterotopic ossification—an abnormal growth of bone—sprouted in his hip, threatening his vital organs and complicating nearly all of his bodily functions. The ossification underpinned a disheartening new routine: head to the hospital for an afternoon scan, end up staying weeks.

People with SCI know their lives are likely to be shorter. Christopher Reeve, America's most famous quadriplegic, died of complications from sepsis just ten years after the equestrian accident that broke his neck. Oftentimes the fight isn't for improvement, it's just for stasis. SCI patients also must navigate a health-care system that is bewildering enough for healthy Americans, let alone paralyzed ones who have often lost jobs and spousal support after their injuries.

Insurance companies don't like outliers. Emmett lives in an apartment, not a permanent care facility, and because by now he's eked out a greater degree of independence than many other quadriplegics, he's something of an anomaly. Other countries don't need GoFundMe campaigns or friend networks the way Americans do. And as is the case with the costs associated with mountain rescues, it's often up to an individual to pick up the post-injury medical tab. Jessi is furious at how her brother has fallen through the cracks. "I mean, it's just challenging for everybody. The health-care system is so broken. The state would pay somebody to come in and turn him every three hours. How are you going to find somebody to come to your house, pay them for half an hour of work? And you're paying $15 an hour? I really don't know how people can navigate the system who don't have support."

After Lauren broke up with him, Emmett dealt with many of these new challenges alone. A few things carried him through the spring of 2019 after Lauren left. He completed a two-week program with a group called Empower SCI, which has fostered the idea that those living with SCI could live independently. For the first time since his accident, the emphasis lay in doing things for himself. He'd previously relied on Lauren, and this program showed him he didn't have to.

The friends Emmett had come to depend on remained by his side. John rented a mountain wheelchair and recruited a group of friends to push Emmett to the top of Mount Sugarloaf in New Hampshire. The gradual gravel path to the summit wasn't climbing, but touching the granite slab on top and feeling the warm breeze and gazing out over the views of the Pemigewasset Wilderness connected him to why he'd loved the outdoors in the first place.

In the main, Emmett has resigned himself to the fact that he will never return to the mountains or climbing, that the challenges he now faces occur in his mind and in his body, not against some dramatic landscape. He compares this reality to slogging uphill at high altitude. Two steps forward and three steps back. "Just this endless plodding along a ridgeline, hoping you get to a summit but you never do. Someday the storm's gonna set in, or nighttime's gonna set in, and it's all going to be over," he says.

In the fall of 2020, as COVID kept the United States locked down, Pat McNally, Emmett's old college and climbing buddy, drove him out to a physical rehabilitation center in Omaha, Nebraska, in the hopes that Emmett would be able to regain a higher level of independence. As Pat and his wife, Cathy, had done many times, this meant assuming complete care for his friend, the nuts and bolts of which are often messy. "I've done things for Emmett I would never have imagined doing for anyone," Pat tells me.

Emmett had hoped the tenure in Omaha would inch him toward a greater self-sufficiency. At first, when I spoke to him that fall on Zoom, he sounded chipper and optimistic. He was learning to use a recumbent bike; the staff were considering how he could use a kayak. Both presented a bridge to the outdoor world that he missed more than anything else.

After a few weeks of not hearing from him, I began to worry. Emmett has a way of not responding when he's in the middle of a setback. When he finally responded in November, he looked gaunt and worn. The sarcasm and witty responses were still there, but he was eighty pounds lighter than when he'd schlepped hundred-pound loads through alder bushes and up steep mountain passes in Alaska in the days before his accident.

"I got COVID," he said sheepishly.

"Jesus Christ, Emmett. Really? Are you okay?" Emmett practically defined immunocompromised. He *was* okay, kind of. There was a digestive complication, another setback to do with his hip ossification.

I asked him if he considered his own mortality differently now. He shrugged. "It pops into my head every once in a while. If something happens. I know people in my condition die sometimes. But broadly speaking, in my day-to-day? I feel invincible again."

A lot of this is just Emmett's personality. If he can't take the weight out of your pack anymore, at least he can laugh and tell you everything is fine. It's how he gives to other people now. Jessi tells me he often won't elaborate what he's going through. He doesn't want her to worry.

I tell him I'd never be able to handle what he'd dealt with thus far. It strikes me that Emmett survives the way people always do in extreme circumstances: by fighting for the small victories and readjusting the lens through which he views success and failure. In a lot of ways, Emmett's strategy for daily life mirrors Charlie Sassara's strategy for getting Jack Tackle off Mount Augusta. Focus on the possible, not the impossible. Don't get overwhelmed by the bigger picture. Keep making decisions.

When John and Alissa finished their year on the road, they relocated to Boulder, Colorado, where John works and Alissa telecommutes. They climb as much as possible, and though both make an effort to see Emmett, these visits happen less often than they'd like. Initially, John and Alissa tried to maintain a relationship with Lauren, but it became difficult. It was as if John and Alissa reminded her only of that long night in the Hidden Mountains. Alissa knows Lauren has valid, rational reasons for becoming disconnected from them. They knew she struggled, yet without Lauren articulating those feelings to them, they were at a loss as to how to help their friend. The relationship became untenable. They hardly speak to each other now.

The nature of John and Alissa's relationship with Emmett has changed, too. Many of Emmett's climbing acquaintances have filtered out of his life. Without climbing as common ground, his closest friends have had to find new ways of connecting with him.

"I mean, it's tricky. You want to say nothing's changed," Emily Matys says. "Obviously he's still our best friend for a reason and I don't think those reasons will ever change, but it's just that everyday life for us is a little bit different."

In July 2021, a surgical team removed the growth that had ossified in Emmett's hip. The removal of a heterotopic ossification is an extremely risky surgery, a procedure done when all other management options have failed. Patients suffer significant blood loss during the operation and recovery is uncertain. Normally taciturn about his complications, the operation worried Emmett enough that he sent an e-mail to me and a few others beforehand. It was tinged with the knowledge it might be the last communication he'd have with any of us.

I'm truly comfortable even with the idea that things might be going less than perfectly because I'm living within the context of an underlying truth that, put simply, every moment I live is an incredible gift and therefore all feelings and experiences, whether positive or negative, are wonderful objective opportunities for me to experience the nuances of life. So of course I'll be nervous, but I'll never for a moment think of it as anything other than a thrilling part of living. I hope that makes some type of sense. It's difficult to articulate. It's also worth noting that this is all taking place after I've come off a very good year. When I think back just 12 months to what my life looked like and the way I was able to think about the future, I can't be anything short of thrilled with where I am today!

The operation lasted all day. A few days later, when I texted him, his surgeon assumed she had been successful. But CT scans soon revealed the growth had returned. He remained in significant pain (it's a common misconception that those with SCI can no longer feel anything). While Emmett recovered in the hospital, David Roberts finally succumbed to his long struggle with cancer. Imprisoned at Spaulding and unable to visit his friend before his death, the loss broke Emmett's heart. Jessi happened to visit Emmett the day he found out. She held her brother tight.

"You can't even support him. And he can't support you the way he'd want to," Jessi says. Yet no one disagrees that the hardships are better than the other, unspeakable alternative. "I wouldn't trade the last three years with my brother for anything in the world."

WHEN THE SUMMER RAINS SOAK THE CLIFFS OF NEW HAMPSHIRE, there's just a single spot in the whole state that stays dry enough to climb: Sundown Ledge, a small swath of granite sheltered by a gentle overhang. Even with water pouring down forty feet out from the start of the routes, several climbs remain dry. And on rainy, humid weekend days it's not uncommon to see multiple climbing parties all hunkered down, sharing belays and laughing and trying and falling, their shouts echoing from the cliff walls.

The routes are tricky, 5.12 or harder, coated with chalk that will never come off, imprints of white slapped on by hundreds of hands. On one of those days in the summer of 2021, I walked through the mist and the thick dark trees and the jumble of boulders, and sure enough, a small group of climbers was gathered. One was Lauren. I said an awkward hello. Alexa knew who she was, though no one else in my group did. I did not want to bring up the book I was writing about the accident. I noticed she wore the same chalk bag she'd had in the Hidden Mountains through that endless night. When we had last talked, she told me that she had not been climbing much, so I was surprised to see her. But maybe, I hoped, climbing was still a salve for her. It was good to know she was here tying in.

Emmett had mentioned they had begun speaking again, and that she visited him in the early part of summer. They'd sat for hours in his apartment, their first meeting in more than a year. What they spoke about remained between them.

We warmed up on a few rock pitches. It felt good to grab the rock, spongy with humidity as it was. Everyone shared ropes and bantered together. The community is still small. A friend belayed Alexa on a route she'd been working for a while and everyone stopped and watched the effort for a second.

Much as Emmett's physical being had changed, I suspected Lauren struggled in ways that were harder to detect. If she felt the guilt I assumed she did, I hoped she'd forgiven herself—a failure to do so would be as heartbreaking as Emmett's quadriplegia. Emmett says he has moved on from grieving the loss of her partnership. "In some ways, it's easier for me. I don't have this level of memory that she has from the accident. And I don't have a choice. These hands got reshuffled and re-dealt. This is the one I got and it is what it is and I'm stuck with it. But she—she has a choice on how involved to be with me. She could just cut the cord altogether." He is glad she hasn't.

It grew dark again. Another round of storm clouds glided across the sky. Lauren and her friends began to pack up to leave and my group walked around the corner of cliffband to say hello to some friends working on a hard, technical line. A few months ago, Lauren had responded to a set of e-mailed questions I'd sent her, though it'd been radio silence since then. At that point, talking about the accident—and what happened after—had become difficult for her to do in person.

"Climbing brought me so much joy, wonderful people, and a sense of direction that was really comforting. The years where climbing was at the center were the best of my life. I miss it all so much," she'd written.

> Since the earliest days in the ICU I knew that Emmett's being alive was extraordinary and it was at the very center of the hope that was literally propping me up minute by minute, day by day. Because his aliveness meant that there was still a chance that he would be alive the next day and the next day and that perhaps eventually he would become alert and then someday we could go home.
>
> Emmett gets so much out of life and he gives even more back. . . . He will always be dear to me. And I am so incredibly grateful he is still here.

I watched Lauren and her friends pause beneath the overhang on the far side of the cliff before leaving, trying to decide when to venture out into the new downpour. The rain came in sheets now. She wavered for a minute before turning toward the trail. Then she cinched up her pack, ducked her head down low, and committed to the storm.

# EPILOGUE

The summer of 2018, on an attempt at a mountain called Latok 1 in Pakistan, a Russian alpinist named Alexander Gukov sent a distress text from the Russian equivalent of an inReach. "I NEED HELP. EVACUATION REQUIRED. Sergey fell. I'm hanging without any gear."

Twelve days earlier, Gukov and his partner, a twenty-six-year-old fellow countryman named Sergey Glazunov, had been the most recent in a long line of climbers to answer the siren call of Latok's North Ridge, a route that had seen scores of attempts by the world's finest mountaineers, and that had nearly been climbed on its first attempt by a team of four Americans in 1978. With each successive failure (nearly fifty expeditions have thrown themselves at the climb), the status of the peak rose to Homeric proportions. Some teams failed to climb above base camp; many were thwarted by the labyrinth of snow features that collapsed and avalanched down the ridge. But on July 13, 2018, Gukov and Glazunov had started up. After six days of toiling through a storm, they'd climbed to a point just shy of the summit. With dwindling provisions and inclement weather, they decided to rappel. As they retreated they began to lose control. At around 20,300 feet, Glazunov made some kind of mistake: either his rappel anchor failed, or he hadn't yet placed one, balancing on the unstable snow instead. Either way, he disappeared down the side of Latok 1. With him went the ropes and the team's rack.

Gukov found himself stranded on one of the most formidable walls on earth without the option to retreat. A helicopter rescue, like Emmett's in the Hidden Mountains earlier that summer, presented the only chance. On assignment for *Rock and Ice*, I had interviewed a few of the climbers who happened to be at base camp. Ales Cesen, an elite Slovenian alpinist who had been waiting for his own attempt on the peak when Gukov sent his text, rejected the idea that a team of mountaineers could battle their way up to the stranded man and make their way back down again. "For us it was never a possibility. Never a real consideration," he'd told me over the phone.

This left a group of pilots from Pakistan's 5th Army and their Euroclair B3 helicopters. The Pakistanis flew into Latok base camp from the Sichuan Glacier conflict, a few valleys away, where they were engaged in active warfare against the Indian Army.

Earlier that season, Pakistani helicopters had failed to reach a dying Polish alpinist named Tomasz Mackiewicz on Nanga Parbat. Back in Europe, the Pakistani government faced criticism for not doing more—a ludicrous accusation, considering Mackiewicz was stranded at twenty-four thousand feet in winter on a peak long nicknamed Killer Mountain. In an added wrinkle, the Russian embassy began applying pressure on Pakistan to rescue the stranded climber, even though Gukov and Glazunov had ducked out of paying the standard $12,000 rescue security deposit when they'd arrived in the country (though this was hardly an exception for small alpine teams strapped for cash).

Despite all this, the most disturbing aspect of the story was the statistic a Pakistani rescue coordinator cited to me: Of forty-four expeditions with permits to climb in Pakistan in 2018, seventeen requested a helicopter rescue. One-third of climbers, in other words—mostly professional alpinists vying for the most extreme routes on earth—had needed support when they'd run into trouble.

"It's hard not to ask the obvious questions," I had written. "Though many of the hypotheticals aren't new, they're becoming a norm instead of an exception to the rule. How do climbers calculate the risk of killing someone during their own rescue? Is it worth risking extra lives to save one already imperiled?"

After six days stranded on the face, the B3 snatched Gukov from his high-altitude purgatory. He was so exhausted he'd forgotten to untie from his small anchor, and for a perilous second, he threatened to pull the helicopter and its pilots from the sky, a moment eerily reminiscent of both Jack Tackle's and Emmett's rescues. But the pitons he'd placed pinged out of the rock and minutes later Gukov was in base camp.

It takes pluck to climb a mountain, but performing a rescue on one requires something different, as the risk you incur isn't based on your own decisions. Dave Breun, the pilot on Emmett's rescue and the copilot on Jack Tackle's rescue, puts it like this: "You start to think, well, why did that guy have to be climbing that mountain to begin with? But that's always an afterthought, when you're thinking about what you just did, and the lives you just risked to save this one. . . . None of us think about those things before we go do it. And it doesn't impact what we do or don't decide to do."

Once contained to well-traveled mountain ranges, rescues like the one that saved Emmett are now a reality on even the most remote peaks. Like it or not, someone's going to try and get you if you're injured or stranded in the mountains. The era of total, mandatory seclusion is long gone. Gone, too, is any ethical argument about communication. Instead, it's time to talk about how to better improve a rescue system that will, if trends continue, be strained to a breaking point. This may be true in Patagonia and Pakistan, but it's also true in the United States.

Marc Chauvin, one of America's most respected mountain guides, offers the analogy of sailors who call for help in the Atlantic. "Aren't they relying on a fairly sophisticated rescue from the Coast Guard? [Climbers] just don't have a coast guard." Not every climbing area lies within a national park. And only two states have a crack crew of PJs and pilots on standby.

These days, rescuers in the United States—professional and volunteer alike—are inundated with calls. "For much of the country's history, this patchwork system met demand," Ali Watkins wrote in the *New York Times* in April 2020. "But that trend has shifted in the last decade."

As more outdoor enthusiasts—climbers among them—head outside, paying for specific rescue teams with specific equipment and training might be the only way to meet this groundswell. In 2017, Americans spent $3.4 million on rescues in National Parks. And, as Marc Peruzzi notes, "That's only a fraction of the country's $400 billion outdoor recreation economy." In other words, it wouldn't be that much of a financial stretch to better fund rescues, given how many people now venture outside.

"It's just pennies," Chauvin argues. "It's barely even a budget item they'd consider in Congress."

This probably won't change until something goes wrong, in the way a highly publicized spate of avalanche deaths jolted a broadening skiing community into taking avalanche awareness more seriously. "If you keep the bar too low, you'll wait until somebody dies to make change. It's almost human nature," Chauvin says.

That said, efficient rescue is just a small part of the solution. As user-friendly as climbing has become, it remains up to the individual to take responsibility for their own preparedness and training.

Hordes of new climbers are striking out from climbing gyms with real gaps in their knowledge base, from both a safety and a recreational standpoint. And on a deeper level, it's imperative that we keep self-responsibility alive. Deciding how much risk we take is on us.

AFTER DAVID ROBERTS DIED, I TRIED TO BRAVE THE TOLLS AND crazy Boston traffic once a month or so and head down to Charlestown to visit Emmett. I'd swing by his apartment for lunch and Sharon Roberts would meet us. The weather always seemed crummy for these visits, though maybe that's just winter in Massachusetts.

Emmett's bay windows overlook Boston Harbor. A recreational marina gives way to the harbor proper and at night the lights sparkle over the docks. Tankers, pulled by tugboats and flanked by harbor police, glide silently past. The neighborhood is quiet. Spaulding lies just around the corner; young professionals jog past in black Arc'teryx jackets and tights on their way to morning coffees or Zoom meetings and people in scrubs and badges bustle across slushy sidewalks.

At first, a visitor to Emmett's apartment might not notice the small things that make this life possible. A mug and utensils with hooks so Emmett can operate them with his hands. The lights that respond only to a command shouted at Amazon's Alexa. Emmett's bulky mechanical wheelchair parked in the corner next to a couch, sedentary so long as he keeps using a manual one. To an outsider like me, peering into a world he cannot comprehend, the distinction between the chairs is trivial. For Emmett, operating his own chair under his own power is representative of a broader sense of freedom. He takes this independence where he can get it. He paid for the manual chair himself—insurance wouldn't cover it—and it had arrived incomplete. Over months, he'd scoured eBay for parts and interrogated physical therapist friends on how to finish constructing it. He's still unsure if he got it a hundred percent right.

Emmett could be in an assisted care facility, and many people in his position accept this as a facet of their new lives. Instead, he lives by himself; a caretaker comes every few hours. This distinction is vital. He cannot control how long he will live. To a greater extent, though, he can control *how* he will live.

A swanky, sun-dappled apartment in the middle of Charlestown is an odd place to find the self-reliance alpinists crave, but here it is all the same. Emmett doesn't get to dictate uncertainty the way climbers do, by making up ethics and choosing when and where they commit to the unknown, but you'd be hard-pressed to find anyone navigating this private wilderness with so much grace. In many ways, hunting that feeling down is why we climb.

A rotating tour of outdoor films, put on by the Banff Centre for Arts and Creativity in Canada, is in town for five days, playing at the Regent Theatre in Arlington.

"You know," Emmett says, "I've got an extra ticket. You should stay!"

Sharon leaves us to it, and a few hours later I am trying and failing to buckle Emmett in for the ride to the theater (Boston has several wheelchair-friendly Ubers circulating the city at any given time). The night has turned terrible: sleet, sliced by streetlights, spits down in diagonal lines. A dark sheen of mixed precipitation glints off the black sidewalk. For a minute neither of us speak as the driver weaves through the Boston traffic.

"Oh, man. I just wish you'd known Lauren before the accident," Emmett says quietly. He still cares for her deeply. Emmett knows everything Alissa and John and the 176th Wing had done to save him. He still thanks Lauren most of all.

"She held me for eight hours." Another pause. "I hope she's okay," he says.

"I hope she's okay, too," I murmur, and it's true. I know Lauren still cares for him as well. She has told me. But if I am honest, I am most worried about the man next to me.

We arrive in Arlington and the driver parks half a block away, the only place where there's a ramp on the curb. Emmett's wheels leave a track through the freezing slop as we meander toward the Regent Theatre. When we get inside the place is packed, although it's the last night of five. As lockdown restrictions ease, everyone wants to be out and about. The glow and heat of the crowd of people hits us. The lost feeling of being elbow-to-elbow hits too. My glasses fog up and we meet some friends of Emmett's and find a place for him to sit.

I haven't had an evening like this in a long time and it feels good, being surrounded by that living, breathing group. Some climbers and skiers and runners I recognize, part of the scrappy adventure community in New England. The lights dim and the Banff Film intro starts to play and soon athletes are BASE jumping and running and climbing and snowboarding on-screen. One paralyzed athlete schusses perfect turns down a British Columbian mountain on a mono ski. I find myself wishing it was Emmett.

Jessi told me that, in some cosmic way, maybe it's fitting the accident happened to her brother. He attacks life with such fierce optimism. He's got all the great characteristics of a mountaineer, and that won't ever go away: a high pain threshold, unrelenting optimism, endless drive. A deep humility. Emmett doesn't know how much more time he has. I suppose that's true for all of us, in less acute ways. Climbing reminds us of that. Sometimes gently. Sometimes not.

I wonder if anyone knows that the guy in the wheelchair in the back of the theater survived something far wilder than any of the footage they've seen on-screen tonight. Emmett had gone to the Hidden Mountains because it presented an adventure in a crowded world. He'd been rescued by loyal friends and by brave strangers who'd refused to give up hope when it had most mattered. He'd remained alive through an inner toughness I'm still trying to grasp. It keeps him alive still.

Emmett waits for the theater to empty before he starts to leave. To someone passing by, his sitting, patient figure must stand out: instantly different. Around him, the audience filters toward the exit, the films reverberating in their heads, and many must be imagining themselves adventuring in unclimbed ranges far from here. In the morning, most of those dreams will be washed away by the torrents of modern life. And perhaps that's what sets Emmett apart. He had dared to go.

Emmett in Gillette Castle State Park.

*(Credit: Jessi Lyman)*

# ACKNOWLEDGMENTS

Books are far more of a collaborative effort than anyone wants to admit. I hardly feel like this one is mine. I owe thanks to many. Here are a few I remember:

First, to the four climbers who entrusted me with this remarkable story. Thank you for candidly reliving moments I'm sure you'd rather have forgotten. I hope I have told your story with honesty. I hope, too, I have conveyed each person's distinct yet collective courage and the remarkable bond you still share. Emmett: If everyone in the world possessed just a drop of your spirit, selflessness, and grace, it would be a very fine place indeed. You embody the best of our sport. In addition, I owe a deep gratitude to the rest of the Lyman family, who took the time to discuss things that were often gut-wrenching, to put it mildly.

Every one—current and former—of the Air National Guard's 176th Wing: Thank you for giving me a glimpse of your world, for answering phone and Zoom calls while stuck in quarantine and on training runs, on runways, overseas, and at odd hours. Though you'd never admit it, you are heroes in the truest sense of that word.

David Roberts did not live to see the publication of this book, but it would not have happened without him. He grabbed me—literally—and told me to write it. When I refused at first, as was typical Roberts modus operandi, he pestered me until I gave in. Until his very last days, he asked probing questions about the manuscript. His encouragement was helpful, and his criticism and honesty were invaluable. I will miss him acutely. In addition, David's wife, Sharon, provides friendship and more insight and observation than she will ever fess up to, something I will forever value.

Though he navigates the glassy walls of Manhattan and not the cliffs of Yosemite or Chamonix, my agent, Stuart Krischevsky, would make a fine mountain guide. From the start, his sound moral compass pointed me in the right direction, and he kept me plodding uphill with gentle, patient, and funny encouragement. In the mark of a truly great guide, he even tricked me into thinking I'd done some of it myself. Laura Ussleman and Amelia Phillips, part of Stuart's team, both read drafts and gave early criticism. I am lucky to have them all.

A huge thank you to everyone at Ecco; though it had no ending, Denise Oswald took off with this rickety book, while Sarah Murphy came in and landed it. Sarah's edits revealed a fascination with the subject I couldn't have wished for in my wildest dreams, and she understood what I was trying to do when I barely did myself. Her measured, careful, and thoughtful edits were the perfect complement to my big-picture tangents and ramblings, and this book would not be the same without her. A huge thank you also to Norma Barksdale, Rachel Sargent, and the rest of the Ecco team.

Jeff Scanlon, you showed me writing is time and sweat and I have not forgotten. Nancy and Jim Carroll, a belated (procrastinated?) thank you for lending me a shed and giving advice well beyond the literary realm. Janet and Freddie Wilkinson lent us a second shed when our need was most dire. Cathedral Mountain Guides let me poach their office to work on the proposal in a shut-